THE UNIFICATION OF GERMANY, 1848–1871

THE UNIFICATION OF GERMANY, 1848-1871

Edited by **OTTO PFLANZE**

ROBERT E. KRIEGER PUBLISHING COMPANY
MALABAR, FLORIDA

Original edition 1968
Reprint edition 1979

Printed and Published by
ROBERT E. KRIEGER PUBLISHING COMPANY, INC.
KRIEGER DRIVE
MALABAR, FLORIDA 32950

Printed in the United States of America.

Library of Congress Cataloging in Publication Data

Pflanze, Otto, comp.
    The unification of Germany, 1848-1871.

    Reprint of the ed. published by the Dryden Press,
Hinsdale, Ill.
    Bibliography: p.
    1. Germany—Politics and government—1848-1870—
Addresses, essays, lectures. 2. Prussia—Politics and govern-
ment—Addresses, essays, lectures. I. Title.
[DD210.P4 1979]   943'.07   78-23470
ISBN 0-88275-803-9

10 9 8 7 6 5 4 3

CONTENTS

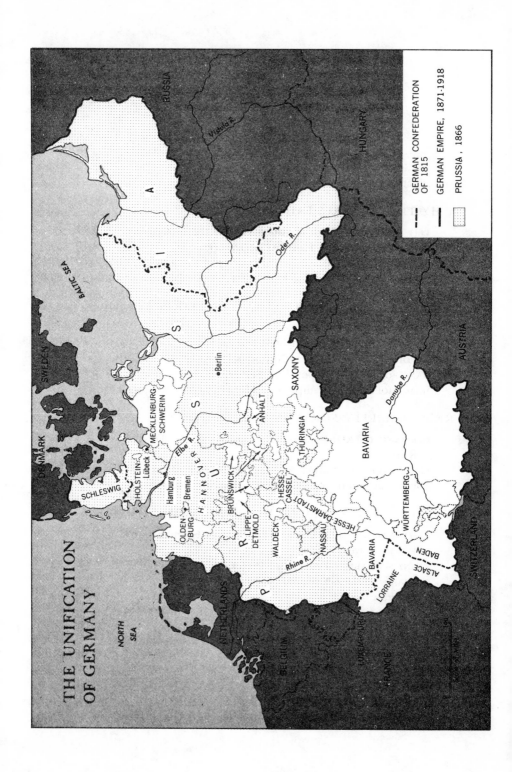

THE UNIFICATION OF GERMANY

GERMAN CONFEDERATION
OF 1815

GERMAN EMPIRE, 1871-1918

PRUSSIA, 1866

INTRODUCTION

A century has passed since the unification of Germany and the founding of the German Empire in 1871. Yet the passage of time has not reduced the number of historical problems associated with these events. During the twentieth century the nation that Bismarck united has menaced the stability of the European order in two world wars, and the German defeat in both conflicts has fundamentally altered power relationships in Europe and throughout the world. Naturally this development has raised questions about the character of the Bismarck Reich and its historical influence. Historians today must cope with the problem of whether this, or an earlier or later, period was crucial in determining Germany's progress toward the cataclysm of our century.

Bismarck's contemporaries also disagreed about the necessity and meaning of what happened between 1848 and 1871. Those who witnessed or participated in the debates of the Frankfurt parliament of 1848–1849, the Prussian constitutional conflict of 1862–1866, and the successive stages of German unification between 1864 and 1871 raised the issues and formed the schools of opinion which for the most part have characterized the controversy ever since. What began as a matter of practical politics has been perpetuated as a problem of historical interpretation.

The Frankfurt parliament of 1848–1849 was split between those who advocated a "Great Germany" (*Grossdeutschland*) and those who advocated a "Little Germany" (*Kleindeutschland*). The former wished to retain the historical connection between Germany and the Hapsburg Empire, while the latter sought to exclude Austria and establish a union under Hohenzollern leadership. The majority in the chamber voted for the *kleindeutsch* solution. The frontiers they planned for a united Germany were—with the addition of Alsace-Lorraine—those that Bismarck later achieved. Historians have subsequently been as divided about the wisdom of this outcome as were the deputies at Frankfurt. Beginning with Heinrich von Sybel, who published in 1889–1894 the first detailed account of German unification, the *kleindeutsch* school of German historians has steadfastly maintained that the exclusion of Austria was necessary. Without it no viable union of the German people was possible. More recent representatives of this viewpoint, whose writings appear in the present volume, are Erich Marcks, Arnold O. Meyer, Gerhard Ritter, and Hans Rothfels. But the opposite interpretation also has its defenders. In four massive volumes published between 1935 and 1942 the Austrian historian Heinrich Ritter von Srbik developed what he calls the "all German" (*gesamtdeutsch*) viewpoint. To Srbik the separation of Austria from Germany meant a tragic division of the German people and the surrender of their traditional role of leadership in the region of central Europe. Recently Herbert Michaelis and Franz Schnabel, selections from whose writings appear in this book, have presented new variations on this theme.

The period of unification was marked by issues of constitutional and social reform. On these problems the revolutionary movement of 1848–1849 divided basically into three groups: moderate liberals, democratic liberals, and social revolutionaries. The moderates, while eager to gain new freedoms, were reluctant to abandon entirely the authoritarian institutions of the past. Hence they arrived at a compromise by advocating a constitutional system of "mixed powers." Essentially, this system called for an executive, appointed by and responsible to the monarch, and a bicameral legislature, whose upper chamber was appointive or hereditary and whose lower chamber was elected by limited suffrage. Since the moderates had the majority, the constitution adopted by the Frankfurt parliament followed this pattern, although the democrats did succeed in gaining universal suffrage. This was the basic structure of the constitution granted to Prussia by the counterrevolutionary government of Berlin in December 1848 and of the more complicated constitution that Bismarck designed for Germany in 1866–1867. Although Bismarck's constitution lacked many liberal features that the moderate liberals considered important (such as a bill of rights and parliamentary control over the budget), they accepted it in their zeal to achieve German unity.

The democratic liberals, on the other hand, were advocates of popular sovereignty. They wanted both the executive and legislative powers in the hands of representatives chosen by the people. Some desired a republic similar to the United States; others would have accepted a parliamentary monarchy on the English pattern. But after 1849 democratic liberalism lost much of its radicalism. During the 1860s its adherents no longer openly demanded popular sovereignty, although they remained staunch defenders of parliamentary rights. Democratic liberals formed the core of the opposition in the Prussian Chamber of Deputies during the constitutional conflict of 1862–1866, when Bismarck defied the chamber by ruling the country without a legal budget. They voted against Bismarck's German constitution in 1867 and 1871 on the grounds that the Reichstag did not have enough power and that there were no guarantees of popular liberties.

At the fringe of the liberal movement in 1848 were the social revolutionaries, who agitated in the interest of the lower classes for social as well as political reforms. In the 1860s their place in the political spectrum was taken by the socialist movements begun by Ferdinand Lassalle and Karl Marx. Under the leadership of Wilhelm Liebknecht and August Bebel, the socialists became the most outspoken critics of the social and political order of the German Reich. Over the decades German socialism, like democratic liberalism before it, tended to lose its radicalism. In the twentieth century its position at the extreme left has been taken by the communists.

These social and constitutional issues survive in the works of the historians. Of the three political orientations, the socialist position is the most weakly represented in German historiography. While important works on aspects of the nineteenth century were written by Franz Mehring and Arthur Rosenberg, there is as yet no major study of German unification by a socialist historian. Since 1945 the orthodox Marxist position has been developed in numerous monographs by Communist historians of East Germany. Their works adhere closely to the views expressed by Marx and Engels, who followed events in Germany during 1848–1871 with keen interest and were outraged that the German bourgeoisie failed to act out its assigned role in the grand dialectic of history. Instead of overthrowing the Junkers, the German capitalists conspired with them against the working class and hence delayed the timetable of the proletarian revolution.[1]

The dominant tradition in German historiography has been that of the moderate and *kleindeutsch* liberals. According to this viewpoint, the failure of the revolution of 1848 demonstrated that there was no other path toward national unity than that which Bismarck chose. The mistake of the revolutionists was to believe that ideas must triumph when their moment in history has come, an illusion that led them to neglect the realities of power (*Realpolitik*). In contrast, Bismarck was a political realist who understood the techniques of diplomatic maneuver and how and when to use force. His success was interpreted as a justification for the autocratic features of the Prussian constitution. Only a monarchical government possessing full authority over the army and diplomacy could carry out an effective foreign policy in a country situated in the middle of the European continent. Insular England could afford democracy; Germany could not.

On the other hand, historians of the democratic political tradition (such as Veit Valentin, Rudolf Stadelmann, Erich Eyck, and Johannes Ziekursch) have never ceased to regard the collapse of the revolution of 1848 and Bismarck's success in the 1860s as a tragedy for Germany. They regret the failure to achieve national unity under a democratic constitution providing either for popular sovereignty or at least for a more powerful parliament and the full guarantee of popular liberties. In their view Bismarck succeeded in pro-

---

[1] For a typical example, see the textbook of Ernst Engelberg, a professor at the Karl Marx University in Leipzig, *Deutschland von 1849 bis 1871* (Berlin, 1959).

longing an outworn social and political order. He rescued Prussian militarism and perpetuated that subaltern spirit in German public life that was its natural concomitant.

The events of the twentieth century have caused other writers to look at popular movements in nineteenth-century Germany more critically. Even those who deplore the political order that Bismarck imposed are no longer sure that the liberals of 1848 presented a workable alternative. Their social foundation was too weak and their liberalism too timid for a successful assault upon the existing order. The nationalistic chauvinism that many displayed was a threat to European stability. For that matter, the subsequent history of nationalism has put in question the validity of the concept of the nation-state. To some, the German Confederation no longer seems as contemptible as it once did, for its destruction meant the end of federalism and internationalism in central Europe and the ultimate triumph of a self-centered nationalism.

Knowing these general trends in the interpretation of German history, the reader will understand why historians take different positions on the issues discussed in this book: the reasons for the failure of the revolution of 1848, the personal and political outlook of Bismarck, the responsibility for the war of 1870, and, finally, whether 1848 or 1866 was the vital turning point in modern German history.

The first section presents the conflict of opinion on the failure of the revolution of 1848. The most exhaustive work on this subject was written by Veit Valentin, who points to a number of factors that weakened the revolutionary movement: internal disunion, social cleavages, dynastic particularism, lack of realism, reluctance to use force, and inadequate leadership. Erich Marcks maintains that the revolution was doomed by the hostility of the European powers. While they did not actively intervene, Britain, France, Russia, and Austria fatally weakened the revolution by showing that they would never permit its success. Rudolf Stadelmann rejected this thesis in a work published on the centenary of the revolution. Austria, he asserts, was the only power that could have blocked German unification effectively, and Austria, owing to its involvement in revolution at home, was as "far away as China" during the critical period of decision in Germany. But could such a complex occurrence as the German revolution of 1848 have failed, as Stadelmann believes, merely because at the crucial moment one man, Frederick William IV, refused to cooperate? In the final selection on this problem Friedrich Meinecke, famous for his earlier works on the history of ideas, analyzes the social character of the revolution. The old regime could have been overthrown, he concludes, only if the revolutionists had been able to unite all the disaffected classes. But those who dominated the revolutionary governments and assemblies feared the lower classes and ignored their interests. They alienated the artisans, workers, and petty bourgeois without whose support they had no hope of final success. What are the implications of the views of Valentin, Marcks, Stadelmann, and Meinecke for a judgment of Bismarck's method of uniting Germany?

Whether the revolution of 1848 could have succeeded under different leadership or other circumstances is a question to which there can be no final answer. Unlike the natural scientist, the historian cannot reproduce the event and, by experimentally altering the ingredients, change the result. Bismarck's unification, however, was not an attempt that failed but one that succeeded brilliantly. Few periods in German history are so well documented as that from Bismarck's assumption of power in 1862 to the climax of 187'. Yet controversies have developed despite the voluminous sources and our detailed knowledge of what happened.

How are we to judge this man who initiated three wars (1864, 1866, 1870–1871) yet afterward successfully strove for two decades to preserve the peace of Europe against great odds? In the second group of selections the reader will see that historians differ no less widely than Bismarck's contemporaries in their answer to this question. To Robert Saitschick, a Swiss writer, Bismarck was a Machiavelli. He unscrupulously violated international law and undermined the European order established in the great settlements of 1648 and 1815. Motivated by Prussianism and Bonapartism, he ruthlessly exploited German patriotism in his quest for power. Arnold O. Meyer takes the opposite point of view. He praises Bismarck for his lack of principles and for the sense of practicality that enabled him to realize the ideal of uniting Germany. He sees Bismarck as a great national hero who brought to an end the long centuries of German discord and weakness, who taught the Germans how to think in national rather than supranational terms and thereby contributed to the peace, not the instability, of Europe.

Meyer's view of Bismarck as a German nationalist has been shared by other German historians, most recently by Otto Becker. But it is challenged in the next selections by Hans Rothfels and Hajo Holborn, who believe that Bismarck's political thought was oriented toward the state rather than toward the nation, (a view expressed also by Franz Schnabel in a later selection). These scholars question the opinion that Bismarck lacked guiding principles or a firm political ethic. Rothfels, who is the author of numerous articles and monographs on the period of Bismarck, maintains that Bismarck's flexibility of method does not mean that he was without any moral convictions or ideals. On the contrary, he was a deeply religious man, imbued by his Lutheran faith with a strong sense of responsibility which prevented him from abusing power. He served the state as an instrument of order in domestic and international affairs, and his freedom from ideology should be praised rather than deplored. Holborn, whose research and writing have ranged from the Reformation to the present, agrees with Rothfels that Bismarck was no mere opportunist and even asserts that he was guided by firm principles, chiefly the need to preserve the aristocratic class and the monarchy from the pressure of popular forces. He believes that Bismarck's religious conversion, while genuine, did not alter his rather cynical view of mankind; furthermore, Bismarck followed the Lutheran tradition in rejecting the possibility that the political world can be improved by Christian morals.

What are the implications of the conflicting opinions over whether Bismarck was a German nationalist or a practitioner of *raison d'état*? Does the answer to this question affect one's judgment of his impact upon the course of German development into the twentieth century? The principal issue debated by Saitschick, Meyer, Rothfels, and Holborn, that of the relationship between power and morality, is a universal one that transcends the career of Bismarck and has significance for our own times. Is the world today any closer to resolving this problem than it was in Bismarck's day? Does your view of this issue as it concerns the present have any bearing on your historical judgment of Bismarck?

Historians are generally agreed that Bismarck, having failed to gain Austria's consent to Prussia's expansion and its hegemony in northern Germany, initiated the war of 1866. Yet the third section shows that there is no consensus on whether he consciously provoked the war of 1870 against France. During the 1920s Hermann Oncken, author of several biographies and monographs on nineteenth-century Germany, collected and published three volumes of documents from German and Austrian (but not French) archives which proved, in his opinion, that the war of 1870 resulted from the centuries-old French ambition to annex the German Rhineland. His introductory essay, from which a selection is taken, was written at a time when the question of German responsibility for the beginning of World War I was a bitter issue. Is Oncken influenced in his judgment of French policy under Napoleon III by his concern over the "war guilt" question of the 1920s? Two decades later Erich Eyck, author of the most detailed biography of Bismarck, concluded that the chancellor intentionally steered toward the crisis of 1870 and deliberately left Napoleon III no recourse other than war. Does Eyck believe that Bismarck was driven to this act by the sheer joy of conquest, by the conviction that France alone stood in the way of Germany's unification, or by domestic problems that required an external diversion for their solution?

Despite the documentary evidence at their disposal, neither Oncken nor Eyck is able to quote directly from his protagonist to prove conclusively the case he advances; both are compelled to argue from partial or circumstantial evidence. Recently the issue of the French-German conflict has been revived by the discovery of additional documents in the archives of the German foreign office. Jochen Dittrich, author of an important monograph on the subject, sees in these sources new proof that Bismarck did not invite war with France. The Hohenzollern candidacy was merely a diplomatic coup intended to produce an internal crisis within France which would leave Germany free to make peaceful progress toward unity. But is Dittrich, any more than Eyck or Oncken, able to produce conclusive evidence for his solution to this problem?

Not long ago a number of leading historians, whose views are given in the last section, reviewed the entire period from 1848 to 1871 in an effort to see its events in the broad context of Germany's historical evolution. During World War II a distinguished British historian of Polish extraction, Sir Lewis Namier, delivered a lecture to the British Academy in which he concluded that aggressive German nationalism "derives from the much belauded Frankfurt Parliament rather than from Bismarck and 'Prussianism' " and that the German liberals were "in reality forerunners of Hitler."[2] In the selection included here he asserts that "with 1848 starts the German bid for power, for European predominance, for world dominion." While finding Namier's thesis exaggerated, Hans Rothfels has applauded it as an important step toward a revised interpretation of 1848. In articles not included here Rothfels agrees that 1848 was a major turning point in German and European history, for it revealed the emergence of disruptive forces—democracy, nationalism, and centralization —which he believes responsible for the ills of our century. These are the forces that Bismarck sought to bind and control by steering against the "current of his times."[3]

Other prominent German historians are less certain than Rothfels of the virtues of the Bismarck Reich. The previously cited selections by Veit Valentin and Friedrich Meinecke reveal this. Valentin portrays the triumph of the counterrevolution and of *Realpolitik* as a tragedy from which Germany never completely recovered. Meinecke believes that 1848 was one of three moments in the nineteenth century when Germany might have fulfilled its "natural task" of transforming the authoritarian state into a commonwealth that would have enabled all strata of the population to participate in the "life of the state." After 1945 Meinecke conducted an inquest into the "German catastrophe" in which he asks whether "the germs of the later evil were not really implanted in Bismarck's work from the outset."[4]

In the next selection Franz Schnabel carries the inquiry a step further by criticizing Bismarck's objectives rather than his methods. The creation of a "Prussian-German national state in central Europe," he argues, accelerated the division of Europe into nation-states, contributing to the growth of international anarchy and ultimately to Germany's isolation in Europe. In rebuttal Gerhard Ritter maintains that no other solution to the German problem was practicable in an age of growing national sentiment. He questions whether the alternative Schnabel advances, that of a federated central Europe, would

---

[2] Lewis Namier, *1848: The Revolution of the Intellectuals, Proceedings of the British Academy*, XXX (London, 1946), 33.

[3] See particularly "Bismarck und das neunzehnte Jahrhundert," in Walther Hubatsch, ed., *Schicksalswege deutscher Vergangenheit* (Düsseldorf, 1950), pp. 233–248.

[4] Friedrich Meinecke, *The German Catastrophe* (Boston, 1950), p. 13.

have had the strength to withstand the pressures from east and west. When, in his opinion, did things go wrong in central Europe if not in Bismarck's time? Herbert Michaelis shares in general Schnabel's view with regard to the ultimate consequences of 1866 for Germany and Europe, but adds a new dimension to the problem by examining that event's effect on Germany as well as on Austria. To him the battle of Königgrätz was a turning point in German history because it deprived Prussian conservatism of its ideological foundation in the doctrine of legitimacy and German liberalism of its last moral bastion in the cause of German nationalism. To be a German patroit henceforth was to be a conservative rather than a liberal. What were the implications of this development for the future?

German historians have been criticized for a tendency to ignore the economic and social background of political events, and indeed the literature on this aspect of German unification has been sparse. The materialist viewpoint has been assiduously cultivated by East German Communist historians. Yet their works have had only limited impact in the West because of their doctrinaire Marxism. Thus far the materialist point of view has been better represented by two Western writers whose historical thought is without this coloration. The French historian Pierre Benaerts, in a book on German industrialization published in 1933, maintains that the economic hegemony achieved by Prussia in the 1850s inevitably led to its political hegemony in the 1860s.[5] In the last selection Helmut Böhme similarly argues that Prussia's triumph over Austria and the lesser states was more the consequence of its economic than its military muscle. By adopting the principle of free trade, Prussia was able to keep Austria, whose industries were weak and needed protective tariffs, out of the German Zollverein. This achievement in 1865, rather than the battle of Königgrätz in 1866, was the climactic moment in the struggle between the dual powers. How does this thesis affect the controversy between Schnabel and Ritter? Does it bolster the case of either? Suppose, on the other hand, that Austria and its German allies had won the war of 1866. Would Prussia's economic might have given it the leadership in Germany if its army had been crushed at Königgrätz?

These many conflicting opinions demonstrate that historical judgments are based on subjective values as well as objective facts. Historians disagree not only because one scholar may know more about the subject than another, but because each weighs and evaluates differently those facts of which both have knowledge. There is little dispute about the details of what happened in 1848, 1866, and 1870, but there is intense disagreement on the meaning and significance of these events. The historian has no fixed point from which to observe the stream of time. He is himself borne along by the current, and his interpretation of the past is influenced by his view of where the stream seems to

---

[5] Pierre Benaerts, *Les origines de la grande industrie allemande* (Paris, 1933), pp. 625 ff.

be headed and whether the apparent destination seems to him good or bad. Although history can sometimes be scientific in its methods, it is rarely so in its results. The relativity of historical judgment, while discouraging, need not be paralyzing. As a humanistic discipline, history confronts us with the continuing task of rethinking the basic values of man's existence, but it also furnishes us with a vast reservoir of human experience from which to draw for our decisions. Even if our conclusions cannot be final, we are ever enriched by the search.

In the reprinted selections footnotes appearing in the original sources have in general been omitted unless they contribute to the argument or better understanding of the selection.

"Watch out that we don't get separated! We're coming to a dangerous point!"
Austrian Foreign Minister Rechberg (*left*) cautions Prussian Foreign Minister
Bismarck in this depiction of their quarrel over what was to be done with
Schleswig-Holstein. The cartoon portrays as well the broader aspects of the
German question: Was there an alternative to unification under Prussia? Was
it necessary or desirable that the historical connection between Germany and
Austria be severed? (From the German magazine *Kladderadatsch*, March 27,
1864).

In two immense volumes published in 1930–1931
VEIT VALENTIN (1885–1947) covers every
aspect of the German revolution. His liberal viewpoint
caused his dismissal from posts at the Berlin
School of Economics and the German National
Archives in 1933. Thereafter he held various academic
and research positions in Great Britain and the
United States. Although he wrote a history of Germany
and a world history, his work on the revolution
is his greatest contribution. This selection is
from the concluding chapter of a translated
abridgment of the original work. His words reflect
the intensity of his emotional involvement in the
events of 1848 and the extent of his disappointment
over the outcome.*

Contradictions Within
the Movement

Bruno Bauer called the Revolution of 1848–1849 "the bourgeois revolution" and thus helped to found a conception which, although completely erroneous, has prevailed to this day.

The designation "bourgeois" has been commonly used for the Revolution of 1848–1849 in opposition to "proletarian" or "socialistic." Certainly the urban middle-class, though in process of decay, stood in the forefront of the movement and its main objective was the reform of the Constitution. But the fate of the population was decided by auxiliary factors, working beside and behind the scenes—the agrarian revolts, the associations of artisans and workmen, the striving after new forms and conditions of

social intercourse in Germany, often with a strong undercurrent of philosophic principles, a sharply critical tendency, a revolutionary inspiration. The battle for a new Constitution was in itself by no means hopeless, and would perhaps have met with success had it not been for the radical minorities whose existence rendered it easier for the forces of counter-revolution to split up and weaken the bourgeoisie. . . .

Naturally there were fanatics and quacks in this German revolution, as in every other. The masses were too enraptured by what was new for its own sake to distinguish the charlatan and the profiteer at first sight. This condition of things most bitterly affected the old

* From Veit Valentin, *1848: Chapters of German History* (London: George Allen and Unwin Ltd., 1940), pp. 422–453. Reprinted by permission of George Allen and Unwin, Ltd.

guard of 1848; their seriousness and experienced knowledge was suddenly challenged and overwhelmed by unbalanced hysteria; disgusted, the former opposition either retired altogether from the scene or sought alliance with the older powers, being usually unable to discern the element of strength in the new, young oppositional spirit.

This procedure meant something decisive in German social history and in the later development of the German party system. Before 1848 there were many signs that a new lower-class might be formed in Germany on a broad basis, consisting of artisans, employees, servants, working-men, peasant-farmers, and small shopkeepers; a class that would have been democratic in the widest sense of the word; that is, national, parliamentary, and social, and which would not have been disinclined to acknowledge a democratic emperor. The Counter-Revolution prevented the development of this class and thus the evolution of such a party. The very name of "democratic" vanished for a time. In South Germany, it was replaced by "People's Party" (Volkspartei). The name and conception "social-democratic," which we have seen appearing in Baden, Saxony, and Electoral Hesse, was destined to a splendid career later. . . .

We must make an attempt to understand the bitterness roused in the lower classes against the moneyed and titled patriciate by their experiences in time of revolution. It was this patriciate which had demanded the leadership of the popular movement and which had now abandoned the struggle. The arrogance of the nobles had been offensive to the small man; but pride of purse and professional pompousness were still worse. The piteous end of the Revolution tended to widen differences between

classes and parties in Germany. The Conservatives rejoiced when the Liberals were reproached with having deserted the poor devils on the barricades and in the street fighting and left them to shed their blood alone. It is one of the strangest consequences of the Revolution that the lower middle classes were politically put to death in Germany. The Revolution had disintegrated them, and as a class they could not coalesce again. It was better, people said, to respect your betters in school, army, and civil authorities, then at least you got on in the world. Intellectual and economic aspects played into each others' hands, to build up a counter-revolution founded on the primal instinct for stability and inaction in the artisan and yeoman.

The revolutionary parties spread confusion among their own followers by their lack of unity, the quarrels among the leaders and the incomprehensible attenuation of their programme. The worst disagreement was between the evolutionary Democrats and the Social Revolutionaries. Often the two parties cancelled one another out on proposed motions, so that nothing at all happened. Discussion was especially fiery in the early days, for it was the new political way of life. German talent for the theoretical celebrated orgies; printed paper guaranteed the immortality of every shade of opinion. The reaction to all this frothiness was the worship of positive power, the "saving deed," everything authoritative which should effectually balance one's own weakness and indecision. The bankruptcy of the Revolution was also a bankruptcy of fine speaking. Oratory had done nothing to alter facts. Nobody had any faith left in [high] sounding phrases. . . .

Germany kept all her Stuarts and

Bourbons; but that European event, the Revolution, left trembling echoes for a long time in royal hearts. There were moody and jealous despots like the rulers of Hanover and Electoral Hesse, fantastically confused absolutists like Ludwig of Bavaria and Friedrich Wilhelm of Prussia. Such personalities could but further the republican idea. But most of the princes showed such utter lack of character, granting at once everything that they had already refused a hundred times, only in order to retain their power, that this at first disarmed the democratic movement. Examples of personal courage were as rare as examples to the contrary were common. False and genial, the rulers quietly prepared for the Counter-Revolution. Some, like Grand Duke Frederick I of Baden, its most successful representative, evolved a new type. They became respectable and middle-class, emphasized their family life, kept their love affairs more carefully out of sight, patronized art and learning as far as respectable and often supported constitutionalism and even German freedom—as long as their royal rights were respected—in a word, they presented the industrious and loyal German of the 'fifties and 'sixties with the very picture he desired to see, since it resembled himself.

Much more serious than the battle against the princes in 1848 was the battle against the petty states. Energetically, and supported by many good reasons, all the frontiers of 1815 were called into question. A caricature very aptly showed the thirty-eight potentates of the Deutsche Bund as cobbling tailors, busily putting patches in the old cloak of the Holy Roman Empire. German Michael[1]

[1] A figure that often appeared in political cartoons, and symbolized the German people. —*Ed.*

was advised to pulp up the old cloak and tailor himself a new one in modern style. There were many beginnings in this question of mediatization, but no end. The idea of the democratic emperor, closely related to the dream of the unified German Republic, really sprang from despair at the realization that particularism was a disease ingrained in the German nature, which broke out afresh in the era of the Revolution and could only be cured by force either of a social-revolutionary or an Imperial character.

All kinds of plans were made, there were even defenders of the petty states. The discussion could not be brought to any logical conclusion. There were as many kinds of particularism as there were types of state in Germany, and they all proclaimed their right to liberty. . . .

National cohesion, a national way of life existed in Germany long before there was a strong national form of existence. Hence the devouring longing of the progressives; they were ashamed to be so rich and yet so unripe. The idea of a strong German nation which was to create its strong empire, filled and pervaded all leading Germans, from Radowitz to Robert Blum, thrusting every other consideration into the background—perhaps too much. The men of the Frankfort Parliament called again and again upon the unfinished Cathedral of Cologne as symbol of the German Empire of the future: one day both would be finished and soar proudly upward. In these days, the belief still prevailed that the German spirit would have the power to break down all opposition.

It was once said most appositely in the Frankfort Paulskirche that it must be feared that the Prussian Diet would prove [to be] the iron wheel in the golden repeater watch of the empire. One could scarcely find an apter metaphor for the unsolved and probably insoluble Prusso-German problem.

It can be precisely observed how the national idea, the great, all-embracing experience of the outbreak of the Revolution, coarsened and lost its ideal character in the course of events. There was something in the idea and in its aims which carried people away and united them; but the paths of accomplishment ran in different directions and even crossed one another. . . .

Comparison with all other revolutions in modern history shows the German Revolution of 1848–1849 to have had the smallest percentage of deeds of violence, also of crimes against property. During his revolt, Friedrich Hecker ran along the ranks, urging his men to take nothing without paying for it on the nail, since the villagers were already lamenting as if a band of robbers were approaching. When, during the Berlin March Revolution, certain people threatened to take a fancy to the silver vessels in the Jerusalemer Church, Wolff the sculptor, who had marched to revolution in his dressing-gown, girt with a sabre and crowned with a flapping broad-brimmed hat, pretended to be seized with revolutionary fury, bore the vessels off and secreted them in his house until things quieted down. There was no organized revolutionary terror; a couple of isolated acts such as the tearing down of the Dresden opera house were mere individual excesses. But there is much evidence that the soldiers beat their prisoners, and the treatment of political prisoners in convict prisons was often purposely harsh.

The German Revolution of 1848 erected no guillotines and held no extraordinary courts of a purely political nature. No one except Prince Metternich was banished; there was no confiscation of fortunes, no holding-up of salaries, no refusal of pensions. No one in Germany thought that in order to combat the past, its representatives must be made personally defenceless and economically impotent. Outwardly it was nothing more than a purely political reversal, borne aloft by representatives of pure humanitarianism; a humane revolution is necessarily a semi-revolution. This was probably the deepest error of the men of 1848. Revolution is battle and carries the principle of force into the formation of the State. The princes had always made their wars ruthlessly without regard either to other peoples or to their own. The German democratic movement of 1848 wished to achieve a gentle victory. No historian will reproach the leaders with shedding too little blood; there are other ways of removing opponents. The Revolution of 1848 did not perceive them or took no note of them. The leaders must have known their opponents well enough, but did nothing to cripple their activity or to replace them in their posts by followers of the new order. The Frankfort central power could have chosen people in whom they could have confidence; but the old particularistic bureaucratic machine continued to rattle untroubled on its way. There were martyrs enough from the Revolution of 1830 and the Wars of Liberation. Certainly they were elected to the Frankfort Parliament—Ernst Moritz Arndt, Jahn, Uhland, Eisenmann, Sylvester Jordan—but they had very little voice in affairs. The young revolutionaries suffered from the German fault of overtrustfulness. They took no revenge; the patriotic and liberty-loving citizens saw the principal danger in the Jacobins, Social-Revolutionaries, and Communists.

Naturally, there was much malicious joy over the fall of the mighty; the lack of talent for quick, sharp action was compensated for by a tremendous gift for scolding: grumbling, criticism, speculations as to how it could have been better done, frittered away the urge to action. Curiously enough, this quarrelsome criticism rapidly turned from the old to expend its force against the new leaders. The new men may have had their weaknesses; but they were mercilessly exposed. The moment anyone rose to the top, he was attacked with embittered jealousy; Welcker, Heinrich von Gagern, Robert Blum, Friedrich Hecker—the same fate overtook them all. This was the reverse side of the medal of the conscientious revolution of 1848; it destroyed its own children. The Revolution had practically talked itself to death by the time the Counter-Revolution was on the march. The people's leaders had only a momentary authority; they had continually to fight for it; their weaknesses were those of the people themselves and therefore unforgivable. Public opinion was particularly resentful if the new men profited economically from their work. Anyone who accepted a government position with a fixed income, like Karl Mathy or Wilhelm Jordan, was already half a traitor. Heinrich von Gagern was so sensitive on this point that it was necessary absolutely to force upon him the salary accompanying the post of President of the Frankfort Parliament by passing a law that there could be no refusal of this salary. A healthy desire to see clean hands in public affairs was thus so exaggerated as to lead to pure absurdity. For the bureaucratic appartus remained, just for this reason, practically unchanged.

Thus the humanitarian State, as the March movement dreamed of it, could not come into being. Men longed for action and feared it at the same time. When the big speeches were over, there was remarkable modesty in deeds and also a certain hesitation. The old layer of officialdom presented a very solid front in comparison. It did not glitter, it did not trifle, it was something in itself and had no need to become anything different. When these people accused the democratic leaders of wanting to snatch office, of vanity and who knows what else, there was scarcely anyone who thought to rebuff the questioner by asking where these noblemen, these property-owners, these manufacturers had come by their fortunes. Most of the new people were poor and suffered from poverty; they therefore hesitated between shyness and excited claims; they had talent, good sense, patriotism, a feeling for what was right; they turned everything into debate, believed they could convince the majority and carried motions; they thought they could alter German realities by a new Constitution, by new laws. It was an honourable undertaking, but unfortunately the mass of the public soon grew tired of it. There was not enough going on, it was not rapid, not dramatic, not wild enough. The loud-mouthedness which sprang up by the side of the noble pioneers of a new justice, awakened in the mass of the public a respect for what had been; pity and sympathy for fallen greatness is also a good trait of the German nature; only a clever twisting of contemporary events was necessary to weld a new loyalty, in exercising which the people thought themselves mighty fine fellows and true as steel. It was just those who had always been despised and ill-treated by the old powers who now made use of the opportunity to get a little nearer to the throne, without running any great danger and so to gain social and economic advantages. The nobles had always had a certain independence; unquestioning devotion was to be the characteristic of this new class of citizen.

The Reform movement had tried to be just to everyone, a political point of view must never anticipate the judgment of history. Will to righteousness made these men self-righteous. This roused their political opponents to absolute hatred. The Republicans, the Social-Revolutionaries, the Communists had the active courage to be unjust; but only minorities followed their lead.

The Counter-Revolution certainly had more courage to be unjust. There was no question of asking whether blood might be shed or property destroyed; there was no need to seize the means of power; the Counter-Revolution had all that was necessary. If the popular movement in North Germany, except in Berlin, seemed somewhat lacking in temperament, the Counter-Revolution was undoubtedly more emotional. Religion, patriotism, morality, loyalty to the traditional ruling house, proceeded to the attack. The Revolution had branded only Metternich as a criminal; the Counter-Revolution branded a whole social class as rogues and vagabonds. When the vanquished marched out of Rastatt, the Prince of Prussia turned away. He did not want to see "such people." The Revolution had built up a legend of its own pre-history; the Counter-Revolution now wrote the legend of the nature of this democratic movement

and thus exercised a decisive influence upon two German generations. The Revolution had taken care to make no martyrs; the Counter-Revolution had no such scruples. Ordinary courts competed with courts-martial. The feeling of justice, so sensitive at this time, was once more deeply wounded by a whole series of political trials.

Jacob Burckhardt said power was an evil thing. There is something worse than power. Power is, above all, fickle. It must be won and manifested afresh from day to day. Only use can keep it bright and keen. It serves only those who grasp it firmly. Woe to them who possess it and do not use it, for it will turn against them. This was the experience of the German citizen of 1848; the measure of logical retribution which he had not in himself, was visited upon him with interest by the Counter-Revolution. The humanitarian, the decent citizen, the cosmopolitan dialectician, had no more to say. The world had shown that it was not beautiful and pure as the classic form, nor joyous and brightly-coloured like an intellectual romantic play. A dashing age usurped the scene, impudent and coarse, unashamed, inclined to mockery and brutality. Certainly no political movement could be suppressed entirely by police and the courts; there were more subtle measures and these had a decisive effect. The "people," it was said, had proved themselves to be insolent, avaricious, rough, and treacherous; they needed control and they should have it. Arrogance and contempt of mankind, the ancient vices of ruling classes, now went disguised as the art of protective government.

The reaction in Germany was all in browns and greys. How picturesque the Revolution had been! Now the best thing was to say nothing more about it;

the very recollection was to be buried. Few of the painters of the time have preserved its gay aspect; the green sharp-shooters with their hunting-knives; the blue militia with light or dark trousers worn with their wide coats, feathers in their hats, cockades, sashes, often broader than necessary, sabres, halberds old rusty rifles as weapons; everywhere the daring, energetic young men, usually in gym-nast's dress, with white, frogged blouses, older men in caps, with long beards, a few gentlemen in blue frock-coats, hunt-ing-rifle slung on their arms, people in all kinds of odds and ends of military uniforms, and finally a sprinkling of Polish frogged tunics. Hosemann's sketches are about the best.

The best of this generation acclaimed a new legal State at once, as a logical and moral postulate and as a work of art. Thus the Paulskirche changed from a sober Lutheran church into a timeless sacred temple, eternal home of the Ger-man idea. On the faces of the men who assembled in Frankfort in May 1848, there was the brightness of such fulfil-ment of destiny. We can still perceive it to this day. But even in this National Assembly, men of such calibre could be only a minority. Next the seers were pedants and fools. Just because the new politicians took themselves with such extreme seriousness, the rebound was sure to follow. Before the tragedy was at an end, the farce began.

In its depths, the eloquence of Hein-rich von Gagern was akin to that of Robert Blum—it called forth the cyni-cism of Detmold and Karl Vogt, so dif-ferent from one another, but united by their sceptical attitude towards all heavy-browed solemnity. Poor Germany, which was also so rich! Beautiful and rich in its landscapes and talents, poor in the results of all this richness, happy in its individuals, and therefore longing for the final depth of individualization, luckless as a whole, confused and put out of countenance by the superfluity, yet tempted again and again to try and master it!

The distance between the two poles of the German being caused the develop-ment of that malady which is perhaps the German's especial curse. Georg Friedrich Daumer considered the events of the European revolution of 1848 to be so monstrous that he believed the "old slavish conditions" under which the German spirit had lived, were now gone for ever and the time had come for a completely new conception of the world in place of the Christian, for the "Religion of the New Age of the World," affirmative, natural, the truly good, and wholesome conception of life and eter-nity. Thus the German spirit again swept forth into the ether at the moment when the practical day's work was most urgent. It strove from the relative to the absolute, it was at once bound to the past and filled with the future, but some-what estranged from its immediate present. German political creation there-fore grew rampantly in space, missing the clear and logical formation of the new, as in France, not drawn to unity by an irresistible popular leadership, as in Italy, nor capable of simple sensible action, wise for the next day to come, as in England, and a Russian intoxication of destruction and creation was equally impossible to it. German political work in 1848 was at once too universal and too specialized—the old powers made the most of this weakness. It is remark-able how the experience of the unity of the German people, the witnesses of which can be seen to-day in any Pro-vincial Museum, could so rapidly recede again, even be almost forgotten. The

German's old inferiority complex was still greater after the Revolution than before. Each kept strictly within his social and professional sphere, the judge consorted only with judges, the professor with professors. Closer than all party formations were the bonds of the clique and the *Stammtisch*, the familiar table at the inn, always frequented by the same few friends. The people broke apart again. There was a temporary end, too, of the self-admiration of the forties. Many had grown humble and willing to be impressed. The Revolution had come to a halt before the thrones and the money-bags—another reason for these two powers to become allies. The immediate future belonged to middle-class militarism. People had seen where a multiplicity of talents led. The superfluity of talents had seized upon everything and with spirit and thoroughness had accomplished all that intelligent patriotism can bring about. There was no strong man, whose personality could have held the thing together. Ideas are good and there had been no lack of ideas, enough to last for two generations. Ideas are splendid, but men are better.

ERICH MARCKS' lifetime (1861–1938) spanned the
Bismarck Reich, the Weimar Republic, and the
rise of the Nazi dictatorship. His greatest interest as a
scholar was in Bismarck, through whom he gained
a respect for the influence of strong personalities
on history. Early in his career Marcks began a
biography of Bismarck, but he completed only the
first volume, published in 1909. The following
selection is from his magnum opus, a two-volume study
of the period of unification, which he obviously
regarded as the most glorious in modern
Germany history.*

The Hostility of Europe

Frederick William . . . was a legitimist. He condemned the revolution and
popular sovereignty from deepest conviction. He wanted to return to the old
Germany, a Germany ruled by the German princes, who alone could summon
him. According to his view the Paulskirche had no right to send him such a
summons. He did not acknowledge that
its constitution had any moral or political justification. The most that he would
concede was the necessity of carrying on
political relations with the Paulskirche.[1]
His royalism and his religious faith led
him to resist even this concession. Yet he

[1] St. Paul's Church was the assembly place of
the national parliament in Frankfurt on the
Main.—Ed.

felt compelled to maintain political contact with the Paulskirche because his
ministers and diplomats urged it and
possibly because he recognized that the
situation in Germany was still explosive.
Under the circumstances it was advisable to create something in order to pa-
cify the population, but this creation,
unlike the Frankfurt constitution, had
to be based on tradition rather than on
human presumption. The question was
how far he could go along with the revolution. In the past he had remained
true to his convictions. Must he not now
continue to do the same? The decision
of his state depended entirely upon him
in such a personal matter [as the acceptance of an imperial crown]. From

* From Erich Marcks, *Der Aufstieg des Reiches, Deutsche Geschichte* von 1807–1871/78
(Stuttgart: Deutsche Verlags-Anstalt, 1936), vol. 1, pp. 312–317, translated by Dennis Showalter and
Otto Pflanze. By permission of Deutsche Verlags-Anstalt.

the start his conscience determined what decision he would make. Two worlds confronted one another; was it not inevitable that they should conflict? The immediate reason for that conflict was the personal outlook of the king. Would someone else have handled the matter differently? Even Frederick William was not without some Prussian pride. Would not a stronger, less inhibited personality have seized the opportunity to put himself at the head of Germany? When exhorted to do so in April 1849, Frederick William made his famous confession: "Frederick the Great would have been your man; I am no great ruler." Undoubtedly, he was incapable of it.

Whether another man in Berlin, a Frederick or a Bismarck, could have seized the reins of the revolution by a grand and daring action, exploiting and at the same time subjugating the movement, and whether such a Prussian policy in Germany would have been possible and successful in 1848, particularly in March 1848, are debatable issues. Like all speculations about events that did not occur in history, there can be no final answers. Frederick William was simply not the man for such a task; his powers were too weak and his convictions too strong. But does the responsibility for the lost opportunity of April 1849 rest solely on one person? Was it a lost opportunity? Did a real chance still exist? This question too cannot be answered unequivocally. The inclination of the critics is to revert again and again to censure of the king alone. Was the fortune of the nation definitely lost because of him? It appears so, but what were the actual possibilities at that time?

Of the various aspects of the problem the one most difficult to determine is also probably the most important:

namely, the *European* aspect. To what degree did the attitude of the European powers influence the outcome in Germany? "The situation is favorable for us," said Beseler[2] on December 14, 1848. "England is well disposed toward us; France is crippled; Russia is afraid that by attacking us it will unite us." At this time King Max of Bavaria ordered his envoys to point out to the great powers, particularly France, the danger that a German empire would pose for the world situation, for the balance of power, and for the treaties of 1815 which the powers had guaranteed. In March 1849, we are told, Austria demanded in London and Paris that a congress of the guarantors be held to consult on all European questions, including the German one. This was perhaps intended more as a tactical maneuver than as a serious demand; nevertheless, it did become known. News reached the Frankfurt parliament of these threatening notes circulating among the great powers. Leaders of the Kaiser party, including Dahlmann,[3] spoke of the matter during the debates. In the *Deutsche Zeitung* in February and March the party "beat courageously on the sword of Frederick the Great"; it did not fear a "baptism of blood" once Germany "had found its leader." Droysen's[4] letters also spoke of the blessings that such a righteous war would have for Germany's internal affairs. No animosity was expected from England; that of France and Russia would be overcome.

The situation was to remain as it was

[2] Georg Beseler, an important figure in the liberal movement in Germany.—*Ed.*

[3] Friedrich C. Dahlmann was a prominent leader of that party in the Frankfurt parliament which wished to unite Germany under a monarchy.—*Ed.*

[4] Johann Gustav Droysen, a Prussian historian and prominent figure in liberal-national politics.—*Ed.*

in mid-summer 1848. England above all wanted peace; Russia threatened; the French press became excited and spoke of the Rhine frontier as soon as there was talk of a German Kaiser. The French government thought of protesting and mobilizing and its ministers declared the issue of German unification to be extremely flammable. The new ruler, Bonaparte, of whom the world and Germany were suspicious, hinted (after April) at the possibility of a Franco-Prussian alliance. The only question was the price. There were difficulties everywhere—in Romania, where the Russians pressed forward, in Italy, and in Schleswig. England and France sought at all points to intervene, to mediate, and to restore. King Leopold of Belgium, fearing that war might cost his kingdom its existence, stood by them and cautioned. Austria was involved in Italy first in a recurring, then in an all-out war against Sardinia; Prussia was more or less certain to engage in war against Denmark. From January until March [1849] the Brussels government urged the western powers to extinguish the sparks in Italy by diplomatic means, but it was finally compelled to let Schwarzenberg[5] go his own way. Since January efforts had been made to find a middle way in Schleswig, but without success. Constant intervention from east and west increased the danger of an outbreak, and at the beginning of April it occurred. This threatened to be the match which would explode the European powderkeg.

The letters that Arendt wrote to his friend Droysen mirror the prospects and expectations. This shrewd political figure—German by birth and sympathy, Belgian by location and political standpoint, and informed by sources in Brussels on international questions—analyzed brilliantly for his old friend of Berlin days the concerns of western diplomacy as they touched upon the German problem. Was the creation of a strong Reich in the middle of Europe, of a Prussian-German unitary empire, which would upset the European balance of power, conceivable without war? From December [1848] on he kept returning to this question. He foresaw that Austria would be vigorous and skillful in opposing this development in Germany and Europe. The discord in Germany would enable the small states, by delaying any final decisions on the reorganization of Germany, to open the door to intervention. On March 2 he calculated what was likely to happen: Denmark would proceed on its course, causing the French, English, and Russians to unite. France would then invade the Rhine and Russia would invade the East. England would establish a blockade and, at best, Austria would be indifferent. Nowhere would there be anything to cling to. For Germany it would be a matter of life and death. Yet Droysen was full of confidence and on occasion was carried away by grand perspectives. Arendt himself urged a sudden action in Schleswig and Jutland. But would Frederick William hold firm? Would he accept the crown at all? On March 16 Arendt wrote that London, Paris, and Brussels were convinced to the contrary. But if he should, Russia and Austria would believe themselves deceived "and conduct themselves accordingly. If he accepts, it would take a miracle to prevent immediate war."

In retrospect, it does indeed seem scarcely conceivable that such giant

---

5 Felix Prince zu Schwarzenberg, minister-president and foreign minister of Austria (1848–1852), under whose leadership the Hapsburg monarchy recovered its power.—*Ed.*

problems could have been solved by parliamentary resolutions alone. The fact that Austria was still involved in the south and, more critically, in Hungary might have meant a delay. Even without Austria, however, the great powers were already raising objections on the basis of their own ambitions and of frictions among themselves. Out of anxiety a Belgian observer might exaggerate the danger of the moment, but the danger as a whole was rooted all too firmly in the relationships of the powers. Among the great powers, England was still the most favorably inclined toward Germany; the English Liberals were not anti-German, and friendly words came from Palmerston concerning German unification and the strengthening of central Europe. Yet England, disinclined to become involved in a European war, was not willing to engage in activity in Germany. As a matter of course it steadily pursued its own power interests alone.

Upon whom in Europe, except a few radicals, did the self-determination of the German nation and of its popular parliament make any impression? As an international movement the liberal democratic "politics of principle" had already collapsed in 1848. Even Lamartine[6] had yielded before the realities of the situation. At that time no people thought of giving help to the Germans. What neighboring countries saw, some as early as 1848 and all by April 1849, behind the claims of the German people was power—Prussian power, a momentous shift in the center of political gravity. That they saw it this way was right and natural. A German genius in Berlin would have had to reckon and negotiate with these world forces as well as with the forces of the German movement. He would have had to play a European game and, in a continent filled with serious frictions among the great powers, it would in all probability have meant a general European war. As matters stood at the time, Germany was alone. It was not supported by a single great power, not by Russia, England, or France. At the most, perhaps, it had the support of France, but only because of the ulterior motives of its president. The eastern powers still stood together, not against each other as in 1866 and 1870. The alignment was difficult for Germany.

The European powers did not intervene. The reason was that the possibility of German unification never became sufficiently acute in 1848–1849 to compel their intervention. The factor of will that could lead to action and therefore to counteraction was missing. The whole world knew that Frederick William IV almost certainly would not act; that much is evident in Arendt's letters. The European reaction became more clearly defined during the period of the Prussian plan for the German Union[7] [1849–1851], as Austria grew stronger; yet, covertly, that reaction was always present. We saw Europe affect the inner solidarity of our revolution in 1848; it constantly influenced the course of events in Schleswig-Holstein as well as internal developments in Germany. If the activity of the European powers in 1848 did not attain a scope comparable

---

[6] Alphonse de Lamartine, French poet and foreign minister of the Second French Republic in 1848.—*Ed.*

[7] The "German Union" was a plan conceived by Josef Maria von Radowitz, minister and advisor of King Frederick William IV, for a federal reorganization of Germany. It was launched in 1849, following the King's rejection of the imperial crown offered by the Frankfurt assembly, and failed in 1851 because of the opposition of Austria, backed by Russia.—*Ed.*

to the values at stake for everyone, that was because Germany itself was not really active. But no one should forget that the European danger, the secret European influence, did indeed exist. We still do not know clearly enough how the German statesmen regarded it; in the case of the Prussian king it may have played a relatively minor role. But his minister openly warned him (March 4) against a new Seven Years' War. And no one could ignore the foreign powers. Europe could not simply look on if matters came to a head in Germany, least of all after Austria's opposition had become apparent. Whoever wishes to recalculate the possibilities of the situation in April 1849 must not overlook these aspects of the problem. At that time it was out of the question that Prussia or Frederick William, surrounded by the great powers, would have been permitted to decide the issue all alone.

Europe aside, how were the forces aligned within Germany? In view of the struggle that would inevitably result from a Prussian-led empire, what solid political forces stood behind the national movement that urged formation of this empire? We have already discussed the intellectual forces, whether friendly or hostile to popular movements, and the lack of mass organizations capable of acting decisively. Since only organized power could be deployed against power, we are concerned here with those previously mentioned forces in German political life which were firm and tangible. Since the summer and autumn of 1848 the steady recovery of the particularistic states—not only of Austria and Prussia, but of all the rest as well—had paralleled the progress of the work on the constitution in Frankfurt. This became apparent in Frankfurt

after the advance of the *kleindeutsch* party had unleashed the struggle for power in the assembly. But wherever we look, throughout the country, the situation was similar. For the moment the small states on the whole, went along with the Frankfurt parliament, while the medium-sized states either went along unwillingly or not at all. And the people? The longer the affair lasted the closer they became attached to their particular states. On the surface, the governments and legislatures were still friendly to the Reich. Yet in Bavaria, despite a liberal-democratic victory in the Landtag elections of January 1849, Old Bavaria[8] stood in a solid front against New Bavaria and both were immediately united in opposition to the proposal for a Prussian Kaiser. The Nuremberg Democrat Gustav Diezel deplored the "tribal prejudices" of even the liberal population. In every little state a naïve particularism emerged. Among the microscopic states of Thuringia a local, dynastic loyalty counteracted the desire for national union. Hamburg, anxious about free trade in Germany and the future of its own free port, turned away from all national goals and resisted any national settlement. Prussia's special pride was nothing more than the same elementary self-seeking on a higher level. As early as December 23, Arendt was especially alarmed over the renewed outbreak of South German particularism and spoke of separatist passions and race hate, of the absence of a true German people. These forces were increasing everywhere. The men of the Paulskirche had not recognized either the strength of these sentiments or the strength of the individual states and dynasties. They set

[8] The region of Bavaria before its enlargement during the Napoleonic era.—*Ed.*

their faith and their will against the evidence of German diversity. Their ardor and their performance become all the more praiseworthy the more clearly one sees the forces opposing them. If they did not become democratic and hostile, these forces grew conservative and reactionary, while the Frankfurt parliament proceeded proudly on its course. The depths were not yet affected by the national current. The German states, Austria, and Europe, were also against it. The forces opposed to the founding of the Reich were already gigantic. Certainly the opportune moment, if there had ever been one, no longer existed.

The centennial of the revolution of 1848, which came in wake of the Nazi defeat, was marked by the appearance of a number of books and articles. Perhaps the best is the work of RUDOLF STADELMANN (1902–1949), who was a professor at the University of Tübingen and is chiefly known for his study of the political views of the Prussian general Helmuth von Moltke. Although he covers the entire range of the problem—economic, social, political, and intellectual—Stadelmann puts the primary blame for the failure of 1848 on a single person: Frederick William IV.*

The Personality of Frederick William IV

The German revolution was heavily mortgaged by the fact that Prussia, through its patriotically inspired but ill-advised step of April 10 [1848] and its invasion of Schleswig,[1] forfeited the sympathy of the great majority of Englishmen. Once again it had fallen upon a weaker neighbor, disturbed the peace of Europe, brought about a general crisis, and created a situation from which there was no prospect of escape. The manner in which the German revolution proceeded was more offensive to the world than the event itself. In the case of Schles-

[1] A Danish attempt to incorporate Schleswig-Holstein into the Danish state led to the military intervention of Prussia and Hanover in defense of the German population of the duchies.—Ed.

wig it succeeded in making even the very questionable legal title of the Danish nationalists appear to be one of the values of European civilization that everyone had to defend. When Prussia, intimidated by the dispatches from St. Petersburg and London, concluded the Armistice of Malmö with the Danish enemy in August 1848 and belatedly submitted itself to an English court of arbitration, the loss of moral prestige could no longer be retrieved. The German failure caused almost open rejoicing in Britain, while its effect on the Frankfurt National Assembly was thoroughly disastrous. The retreat of Prussian Staatsräson led to a wild outburst of chauvinism, particularly from the extreme Left.

* From Rudolf Stadelmann, *Soziale und politische Geschichte der Revolution von 1848* (Munich: Verlag F. Bruckmann, 1948), omitting most of the original footnotes. Translated by Dennis Showalter and Otto Pflanze. By permission of Verlag F. Bruckmann.

The debates on the Schleswig-Holstein question in the Paulskirche showed that the enthusiasm for nationalism did not come from the moderate center and the kings, but from the bourgeois radicals, who were already accustomed to thinking in terms of the masses and calculating on their emotions. The most inflammatory expression of German anger and of the German idea of honor in the Schleswig-Holstein affair was uttered by the Silesian democrat Heinrich Simon from Breslau, whose tone was like that of the demagogic agitators of the twentieth century: "If Russia, France, or England should dare to interfere with our righteous cause, we will reply with 1,500,000 armed men. I say to you that neither Russia, nor France, nor England will risk it, and I want to tell you why. . . . Because they are smart enough to know that if they attempt an unjust attack on Germany it will lead to a German national uprising such as the world has never seen."

This outburst of German national sentiment and the resulting conflict with the European powers might have been avoided if Prussia, from the beginning of the Schleswig-Holstein affair, had relied on English assistance and sound diplomacy instead of seeking popular approval. After acting as mediator in the German-Danish border question, England might even have been ready to assume the guardianship of the emerging German national state. . . .

At this moment Austria was as far away as China. Neither the cabinets of Europe nor the governments of the German states seriously included it in their calculations, and the old German question of Prussian-Austrian dualism was practically nonexistent in the spring of 1848. The uneasy princes in southern and central Germany all felt that their only remaining choice was between a

republic and Prussian leadership. Along with their moderate "March cabinets," they were ready to follow a vigorous course set by Berlin, as long as it adhered to the bourgeois-constitutional line. The obstacles lay chiefly in Berlin, where the ministers were dilatory in grasping this great opportunity and remained internally divided at every stage. A great liberal statesman did not emerge, and the leading ministers, from Bodelschwingh to Auerswald, were weak personalities unable to prevail against the resolute Old Prussians, who with their Petersburg comrades believed that the situation could not improve until the army was ordered to shoot at the masses. Between them stood Radowitz and the king, with their romantic plan for a *grossdeutsch* dualism, and Herr von Arnim, with his unfortunate view that the confidence of the nation could only be gained by energetic action in Schleswig-Holstein.

So the offer of mediation casually made by England was not seized and the great opportunity was missed. Recently historians have attempted to justify this failure. It is maintained that the fate not only of the campaign against Denmark, but of the revolution and of German national unity was sealed by the opposition of the European powers.[2] Indeed, the chief foreign threat to the

[2] Erich Marcks began the discussion with his suggestive essay, "Die europäischen Mächte in der achtundvierziger Revolution," *Historische Zeitschrift*, vol. 142 (1930) and with the analysis in the first volume of his historical work, *Der Aufstieg des Reiches* (Stuttgart, 1936). The thesis was developed most fully by Alexander Scharff, *Die europäischen Grossmächte und die deutsche Revolution, Deutsche Einheit und europäische Ordnung, 1848–1851* (Leipzig, 1942). Two further essays by the same author, in *Kieler Blätter* (1942) and in the Festschrift for Karl Alexander von Müller, *Stufen und Wandlungen der deutschen Einheit* (Stuttgart, 1943), pp. 196ff., are concerned particularly with the Schleswig-Holstein question.

emergence of a more closely united German confederation, led either by Berlin or Frankfurt, lay in the possibility that the eastern and western great powers would ally to prevent the rise of a new power in central Europe. To be sure, France and Russia were divided by deep ideological, political, and sociological differences. The question was whether a common anti-German interest would enable them to bridge these differences. Was it possible that a republican and a tsarist government could ally if the movement for German unity should become stronger and gain the encouragement of England? . . .

A French-Russian alliance became a real possibility only when the most sensitive political issues were raised; namely, those affecting Poland and Schleswig. It would have required massive disturbances on the part of Germany to produce a military cooperation between these powers. French foreign policy remained passive on the whole, while in Russia there was no desire for war and even a great aversion toward it. A pliant and cautious stance in foreign affairs by a united and liberal German state would not, as far as we can judge, have drawn the two neighboring powers together. Russia was happy as long as the Germans and the Poles were not brought together by their common drive for freedom. However, that was hardly to be feared after the local battles between Germans and Polish insurgents in Posen had considerably reduced, especially in northern Germany, the German enthusiasm for the Poles. Once the province of Posen was divided into a German zone and an autonomous Polish zone, Russia could hope to occupy the latter without using force. This expectation had a decidedly calming effect on Russian policies.

Considering the matter from all standpoints, it can be said that the foreign powers, while contemplating the formation of a German state with some misgivings, would never have hindered it if it had been accomplished within the region of *Kleindeutschland* and without disturbing the frontiers of other states. England itself would not have been unhappy to see German Austria separated from the Hapsburg territories. This would have weakened Austria's position both as a world power and as Russia's partner on the chessboard of European politics, and the new Germany, led by Prussia, would have entered continental politics as the liberal partner of England. Hence conditions on the European scene were not unfavorable to the creation of a moderate German constitutional state. If this German national state did not emerge, we shall have to seek the cause not in the hostility of Europe but within the revolution itself. . . .

All the charges leveled at Prussia cannot obscure the fact that it alone had the power to put into effect a German constitution based on bourgeois-liberal principles. The central problem of the revolution was not whether Germany was to be a republic or monarchy, a federal or unitary state, or even whether its frontiers were to be *kleindeutsch* or *grossdeutsch*; it was the relationship between Prussia and the Reich. This very problem still burdened Bismarck's creation in 1871 and was not settled even during the Weimar Republic. In all probability there was a better chance for its solution in 1848, when liberal doctrine was dominant, than later under the hand of the Junker from the Mark, who was contemptuous of ideas. That the German people did not gain a satisfactory solution to the Prussian-German question in 1848–1849 was largely due to the romantic notions and the personality of Frederick William IV. The autocratic enthusiasms and fantasies of this unstable king were almost as pernicious for our national development as the romantic militarism of William II and the romantic racial doctrines of Adolf Hitler. The Prussian king, who had promised to lead Germany and bring honor to the black, red, and gold flag, instead destroyed the fruits of the abortive German revolution and even squandered the small gain that could have been achieved by sparing princely sovereignty and securing the consent of foreign powers. The fact that Frederick William failed to rise to the occasion for reasons of conscience rather than ineptitude does not diminish the fateful consequences of his behavior. He was not only the destroyer of the German constitution, but also the gravedigger of German unity.

FRIEDRICH MEINECKE (1862–1954), probably
the most influential German historian of his time,
was long associated with the University of Berlin.
Editor for many years of the journal *Historische
Zeitschrift*, he is chiefly known for his perceptive works
in the field of intellectual history, including
studies of the emergence of nationalism, historicism,
and the concept of *raison d'état*. In the Hegelian
tradition, he first saw the revolution of 1848 in terms
of the movement of liberal and national idealism.
Toward the end of his career, however he came to the
conclusion that economic and social factors were
vitally important in determining the course
of the revolution and its outcome.*

Lack of Unity Among Disaffected Classes

We must set before ourselves today more sharply than before, the problem of critical alternatives in the history of Germany, in order to gain a deeper insight into the infinitely complex web of her dark destiny. The natural task of Germany in the nineteenth century was not only to achieve unification, but also to transmute the existing authoritarian state *(Obrigkeitsstaat)* into a commonwealth *(Gemeinschaftsstaat)*. To that end, the monarchical-authoritarian structure had to be made elastic—if possible, through peaceful reform—so that the result would be an active and effective participation of all strata of society in the life of the state. This was imperatively demanded by the new configura-

tion which was in process within the German society, and which was undermining the former aristocratic foundations of the authoritarian monarchy. An upper middle class arose, the lower middle class increased in large strides, and the beginnings of the industrial proletariat in the middle of the century gave notice of its mighty growth to come. Now, the task of reorganizing and harmonizing within a new commonwealth a people in social transition, bursting with vitality, remained largely unfulfilled, although many liberal and democratic concessions were granted by the old authorities. Which then were the decisive points in this development? When were possibilities first seen, at-

* From Friedrich Meinecke, "The Year 1848 in German History," *Review of Politics*, vol. 10 (1948), pp. 475–488. Reprinted by permission of the Review of Politics.

tempts made or frustrated, which could have brought Germany forward upon the path to the commonwealth?

I see, above all, three such moments. The first occurs toward the end of the Prussian era of reform, in the year 1819 —the year of the Carlsbad Decrees— when with the dismissal of Wilhelm von Humboldt and Boyen, their most fruitful constitutional projects were also buried, and the authoritarian and militaristic principle triumphed in Prussia. The second crisis, when this principle once more won out in the end, was the year 1848. And the third point of decision was the Prussian era of conflict and the year 1866, which, while seeing some progress made toward satisfying the desire for national unity and strength, allowed the liberal and democratic ideas only a partial or apparent success. For it separated the way of the upsurging popular movements from the authoritarian-militaristic citadel of the entire national life.

Of these three fundamental decisions of the nineteenth century, the first was fought out in the more restricted circle of the ruling class itself, between high-minded and farsighted statesmen on the one hand and a monarch of limited understanding on the other. The third crisis developed as a duel between the liberal upper middle class and Bismarck, in which that tremendously skilful campaigner understood how to win over at last a large part of the opposition. At no time in the years before 1866, was the weapon of a revolution seriously considered by Bismarck's progressive antagonists; they were fearful of it, in accordance with the instincts of an upper bourgeoisie. The second crisis—that of 1848—offers therefore a unique, and for us today, a moving spectacle: here the whole people, not Prussians alone, but Germans of every class, stepped into the arena, and an actual revolution came about.

Revolutions, fearful as the invasion of irrational forces may be, or turn out to be, have in certain cases their deep historical justification. Such was the case in Germany, and especially in Prussia, in the year 1848. Admittedly the old order, now attacked by the revolution, was not in all aspects characterized by decay or ossification. The *Biedermeierzeit* with its lovely spiritual flowering had gone before. The Zollverein, since 1833 a work of the Prussian bureaucracy, had made secure the indispensable preconditions for the rise of modern economic forces, and thereby also for the social transformation from which the revolution itself had sprung. The psychopathic romanticist who now sat on the throne of the Hohenzollerns [Frederick William IV] was himself inspired with a deep love for German civilization (*Deutschtum*), and was at some pains to bring about a German unity in its own way. But this way contradicted most sharply the urgent needs of the time. It was upon illusions that he based his attempts to reform the wretched organization of the German Bund and to fulfill the promise of a constitution (made in 1815) by the assembling of the united provincial diets in 1847. For the strongly aristocratic composition of these provincial estates, and the narrow powers which were all that the king would concede to them, were completely inadequate to satisfy the claims of popular representation which grew out of the process of social change. And in everyday life one felt everywhere the old absolutist-militarist police state, unbroken in spite of the isolated concessions to liberalism which the king, giving with one hand and rescinding with the other, might make. But behind the reaction against his personal and self-contradictory rule, and behind all individual grievances, there stood as a deepest source of discontent the feeling that the Prussian military and Junker state must be reorganized from the ground up—that the old authoritarian state must give way to a new commonwealth.

In fact this emotion, spurring on toward revolution, was not actually evoked but only powerfully stimulated, by the February revolution in France and the scattered revolts that were flaring up throughout Germany and even in Metternich's own Vienna. The remarkable circumstance that everywhere they succeeded at once, without encountering resistance, would demonstrate that the moral position of the rulers themselves was already noticeably shaken, that they no longer possessed an unquestioning and naïve faith in the viability of the old order. Such a faith was necessary, if the governments were to use against the revolution the physical instrumentalities of power, still amply available to them. When later they realized that these resources were still at their disposal, the authorities did not hesitate to act accordingly, and to suppress the revolution with reaction. But as things were in March, 1848, they all, as Frederick William IV later expressed it, "lay flat on their bellies."

He, the king himself, most of all. And this in spite of the fact that he had actually launched, on the 18th of March, the physical auxiliaries of his power—his faithful army—successfully against the people's barricades in Berlin. Yet on the very next day, he permitted, through his own order, these troops—though undefeated—to abandon the inner city which they had conquered, and thereby exposed the person of the king to the severest of humiliations at the hands of the rebels. Let us leave aside entirely the tangled complexity of these events, which have been investigated time and again, and emphasize only this. So feeble and contradictory a policy could not have been conducted by any prince, who, with a pure and undiminished faith in his old world, was simply defending it against a new. This new world had already to some degree insinuated itself, secretly and unsuspected, into his own thinking, distracting and weakening his power for effective action. Sooner or later the new was bound to win out, in spite of many setbacks to come, and to replace the authoritarian state by some form of democracy.

Such an interpretation may be justified, as we look back over the whole century that separates us from the year 1848, and as we think of the task now before us—the task of casting aside all relics of the authoritarian state (of which the Third Reich was, in fact, but a malignant outgrowth), and building up a sound and vigorous democracy. The easy victory—to be sure, not a military but a political and psychological victory —by which the street-fighting in Berlin prevailed over the old military monarchy, suggested symbolically that the latter's downfall was written in the stars; that one day the sovereignty of the people would become a reality. But, at the same time, it was no more than a symbol. For the new world was as yet quite untested and immature, and the old world still possessed many unexploited resources—even the chance of remaining victorious for some time to come. Bismarck and his work, after all, had sprung from it, at once magnificent and ephemeral. But let us now mark clearly the indications of that immaturity in which the new world of democracy then continued to find itself.

First a glance at Berlin. The men on the barricades of the 18th of March certainly fought bravely and fiercely, more fiercely than the Parisians before them had fought on the 24th of February. Such was the opinion of the Frenchman Circourt, who had come to Berlin as the representative of the new republican government, and had witnessed both engagements. But was it really the whole of the Berlin populace that stood behind the fighting or accompanied it with good wishes? Pastor Bodelschwingh, son of the minister whose task it was to pass on the royal command for retreat on the 19th of March, wrote in 1902:[1] "We youngsters were running about on the streets that Sunday morning (March 19). With the uprising repelled, there reigned a joyful mood among the greater part of our population; everywhere from the houses the troops were plied with food." Of course, most of the individual bits of evidence which we possess concerning the 18th and 19th of March, are colored to some extent by the sympathies of the witness, and so this testimony of Bodelschwingh should not be taken too literally either. But even less does it deserve to be entirely discarded. And a glance at the general attitude of the German upper middle class in the years 1848–1849 reveals all the more clearly that large sections of this class were still greatly desirous of tranquillity, and continued to be loyal to the old authorities.

---

[1] Pastor Bodelschwingh is known as the founder of Bethel. The author wrote to him in 1902, requesting information about the revolution of 1848; the above quotation is from his reply.

It is necessary to go more deeply into these questions, in order to explain the paradoxical fact that the German revolution of 1848 could everywhere succeed so easily at first, and then in the sequence of events be overthrown with comparatively little effort. To understand this, the character, attitudes, and moral habits of the German people as it was at that time, and those of the various social strata within it, must be taken into consideration. And our contemporary need to attain to an inner relationship with this first attempt at Germany democracy gives this problem all the more importance.

The German people had only just emerged from the years of thinking, writing, and striving. But the thinking and dreaming continued likewise within the framework of new achievements and new desires. This ideological groundswell is common to all parties and classes within the German people, from Frederick William IV and his devout Christian-German friends—the extremists of reaction—all the way to the extremists of revolution: the men whose forceful minds conceived the Communist Manifesto of 1848, Karl Marx and Engels. For did not Hegel live on with them—a Hegel in reverse and yet preserved (*aufgehoben*)? Was it not true of both these thinkers, who claimed to regard all ideologies as merely secondary efforts of fundamental economic forces, that in them there came to life something distinctly ideological—an unqualified belief in the determining power of the laws of development—set up at a time when they themselves found only a tiny handful of followers? In any case, we ought no more gainsay the strong impulse of idealism which worked in these men, than that operating in Dahlmann and Gagern—the champions of the liberal nation-state—or in the brothers Gerlach, defenders of a divinely ordained corporative state. The German revolution of 1848, admittedly, shows not only an all-pervading spirit of idealism, which often outstripped reality and became ideological. It also brought to bear what in actual effect was more powerful—the reality itself, the massive and elemental interests of individuals and social groups. And, because it *was* a revolution, it likewise saw the release of base passions, and outrages of all kinds, perpetrated by the Right as well as by the Left. But if 1848 is compared with other revolutions—and particularly with the most ignominious of all revolutions, that of 1933—it can be stated that the factor of human depravity played a comparatively insignificant role. This must not be obscured by the fact that the extremist parties took pleasure in accusing one another of disgraceful conduct. Theirs were for the most part "atrocity stories." Neither was there anything which could be termed a "brutalized soldiery," nor were the barricades and the free corps of Hecker and Struve manned by a mere "mob." The German people, considered as a whole, kept in those days to a comparatively high moral level.

It must be admitted that their level of life no longer possessed the spiritual grandeur of the age of Goethe. This decline was unavoidable in any case, since the urgent task of establishing a new political and social way of life compressed men into mass or group patterns, and made it more difficult for the individual to gather within himself the creative force from which proceeds all great culture. But what mattered now was, whether this people would prove to possess the maturity, the strength, the insight and steadfastness, that its new

task demanded. Certainly, as we have noted, it was written in the stars that one day the new world would triumph over the old, popular sovereignty over the authoritarian state. But could the victory be achieved at this juncture? The fact that the revolution failed does not necessarily prove that the people were not ready; this may have been due to the coincidence of accidental factors. How bitter were the complaints, in the very midst of events, that just such a personality as Frederick William IV should have been for the revolution its "man of destiny"—a man who had actually, out of weakness, bowed before it at the outset, but who had then stubbornly resisted it; and by his refusal of the imperial office on April 3, 1849, had allowed the nation's call for the creation of the liberal nation-state to die away. Certainly another man in his place could have attempted another and possibly more propitious solution of the German problem. Then, however, the success of the attempt would once more have depended, in the last analysis, upon the world situation. This aspect of the problem we shall take up later. Suffice it now to ask again: was the German people really prepared for the task ahead?

Basic attributes and historical experiences, working together, had made the German people parochial, not only outwardly but inwardly as well, to a degree hardly equalled in any other nation of Europe. The princely territorial state, multiplied a hundredfold to the point where it exhibited absurd extremes of dwarfishness, depended everywhere upon a landed gentry which served the state and, in return, held sway over those beneath them. All this had mingled with the German bloodstream and had rendered the German people obedient and lacking in political self-reliance. In this very multiplication of authority, we see the chief means by which the mentality of the authoritarian state penetrated so deeply into the pores of German life.

One need only compare this with the development of England and France, where the royal absolutism—in England short-lived anyhow—had indeed helped to create a unified nation, but had never been able to instil so lasting and thoroughgoing a habit of obedience, as had the multiplicity of small German principalities. How far an original or native trait had helped to bring this about, can only be conjectured. Was it perhaps the spirit of fealty described by Tacitus? But the example of the Germans in Switzerland and their historical development since the Middle Ages indicates that there were other potentialities of a political nature inherent in the German character. Free of princely and therefore of rigid rule, subject only to patrician and—by the same token—more pliable authority, Switzerland was enabled to develop the native democratic tenet of her original cantons into the governing principle of her commonwealth, and thus to build upon historical foundations a modern democracy. No, the German need not submit to any fatalistic dread that because he is a German, he may for ever and ever be condemned to the habits of servility implanted by the authoritarian state. But it takes time, much time, again to tear free of it. Then too, this state has borne the German people, along with evil fruits, many and varied benefits, and thus fashioned much of ethical value that might well be carried over into the new world of the democratic commonwealth.

Good and evil alike, then, grew out of this disposition toward obedience, whose origin may well be placed primarily in the political fragmentation referred to above. Even where a larger political entity was growing up, as in Prussia, the extreme insistence upon this subservient attitude brought out in a manner especially striking the contrast between its good and evil effects. Prussia was, indeed, a state with two souls: the one austere and narrow, withdrawing into itself; the other culturally alive, striving, in Boyen's phrase, toward a threefold alliance of *"Recht, Licht und Schwert."* This Prussia, at once forbidding and attractive, now exerted her influence upon the rest of Germany. But how much was this influence again bound to confuse and distract all the aims of revolutionary Germany! The singleness of revolutionary purpose which would have been necessary for a victory over the old order, was thus rendered at the outset far more difficult to achieve. Now the German people, breaking loose from its previous subservience, did indeed reach out tumultuously for unity, power and freedom—only to find itself divided anew when it sought to determine the methods by which these were to be accomplished. How deep was the disintegrating and paralyzing effect of the Austro-German (*grossdeutsche*) problem, which implied what to some seemed an avoidable, to others an inevitable sacrifice of a portion of their fellow-countrymen (*Brudersstamm*), and the break-up of a German national community; how strongly has this problem contributed to the negative result of the revolution! It is hardly necessary, in addition, to recall the particularism of the intermediate German states. In fact, it was not merely the egotistic instincts of the princes, of their court councillors and court provisioners, but particularistic tendencies as well, conscious or unconscious, in the

people themselves, which came into conflict with the new yearning for unity.

These were the factors of secular
growth, going back as far as the Middle
Ages, which weakened and divided in
advance any unified revolutionary purpose in the German people. To these,
however, were now added problems of
the most modern type, arising out of the
new configuration of society. It is true
that the one part of the people which
now broke away from the old attitudes
of obedience, and rose up against the
authoritarian state and against the
splintering apart of the nation, was
agreed upon the demand for greater
unity, power and freedom; but it fell out
once again over the emphasis and interpretation to be placed upon one or another of these three words. For behind
the national revolution there was un-
folding a social revolution, a class struggle between the old, the newer, and the
newest social strata. This fact was recognized most clearly at the time by
Marx and Engels, the champions of the
newest class—the industrial proletariat
—which had only just arisen and was
still by no means very numerous. Between this youngest and (as Marx and
Engels dogmatically proclaimed) poten-
tially most important class, and that
which had ruled so far—the nobility
and the higher bureacracy—there lay the
two clearly distinct divisions of the
bourgeoisie: the upper and lower middle class. The first was of more recent
origin; the other dated far back, though
it was not nearly as old as the peasantry
—who, together with agricultural labor-
ers, still made up by far the preponder-
ant majority of the people as a whole.
(The committee on economic affairs of
the Frankfurt Parliament estimated that
they constituted virtually four-fifths of
the total population at that time.) The

share of the rural population in the revolution was certainly not unimportant,
but created no particularly complicated
issue for the fate of the revolution as a
whole. Since a general land reform
through the dismemberment of the large
estates was not yet seriously envisioned,
the agrarian problem of 1848 entailed
only the casting-off of all remaining
feudal encumbrances upon the peasant
class and the peasant holdings. That
was a comparatively simple task. Even
conservative statesmen realized the necessity of solving this question at once,
and when the peasants saw that steps in
this direction were being taken or being
planned, they calmed down again. They
still shared sufficiently in the old habits
of subservience, in any case. The young
Bismarck could well consider using them
as tools in the counter-revolution.

Side by side with the working class,
the lower middle class provided most of
the revolutionary energy. Craftsmen and
workers formed the bulk of the fighters
on the barricades. Had they not risen
up, the revolution could not have
achieved dynamic force at all, and all
the idealists and theorists of the general
movement (reaching into the upper middle class) would have remained officers
without an army. There would have
been no parliament in the Paulskirche,
no draft for a German constitution with
an hereditary Prussian emperor at its
head. The craftsmen in Germany at that
time were badly off. It was related in the
Paulskirche that there was one small
town with seventy tailors, of whom only
seven were able to find employment.
Some hardship was caused by guild re-
strictions which continued here and
there. But a genuine guild spirit revived
again, as is evidenced in the desperate
struggle waged against the new machine

by workers who were losing their livelihood, in the excesses committed by the waggoners against the railroads and by the boatsmen against the Rhine river steamers. These were all, in fact, merely symptoms of the basic feature of an age in which the machine, and the modern technology, had revolutionized the entire life of the western peoples, by creating new human masses and new, unsuspected and distressing situations among these masses.

In such a crisis, the old authoritarian state proved unable for a long time to provide effective aid. Its officialdom was vacillating between benevolence and a narrow, pedantic attitude; its police a nuisance; its army—though possessed in the militia (*Landwehr*) of a more popular aspect—aroused bitter opposition by the arrogance and drill-ground manner of the regulars and their officers. Democracy as a cure for all these sufferings was the magic word that echoed through the ranks of the lower bourgeoisie—a class so quietist by nature and so restless now. The working classes took up the same slogan, and added to it their own socialistic demands. The younger generation within the upper middle class in many places espoused the democratic cause with enthusiasm, and imbued it with the impulse of idealism. It was, to be sure, an exceedingly immature and primitive democracy of which these Germans dreamed, more a rejection of the old authoritarian state than a positive affirmation of the people's state resting upon a fully developed common spirit among all classes. The distrust and arrogance with which the various classes regarded one another, once more divided the very groups which had just made common cause against the old authorities. Let us illustrate this and

other facts aforementioned, with certain experiences which the young Rudolf Virchow had in the March Days of Berlin.

Eight days before the 18th of March, he had returned from Upper Silesia, where he had been sent as a doctor to study the "hunger-typhus." He was indignant at the inability of the magistrates to take effective measures, and had long been convinced that the absolutist system of government was untenable. He assisted in the building of barricades on the 18th of March, and, armed with a pistol, placed himself at the one which blocked the Friedrichstrasse from the Taubenstrasse. Only six days later, he had to admit in a letter to his father: "Already there begins a reaction among the citizenry (Bourgeoisie) against the workers (the people). Already they are speaking of a rabble, already plans are being made for withholding equal distribution of political rights among the various groups in the nation." But, he added, the popular party would be alert and powerful, and would see to it "that no bourgeoise should enjoy the fruits of a battle it had not waged."

One realizes here the closeness of the relationship between events in Berlin and the revolutions of 1830 and 1848 in France. But the problems of the German revolution were nevertheless much more complicated than those of the French uprisings. For the social revolution in Germany and its underlying class struggle was interwined with the national revolution in a way which finally led to the failure of both. France no longer had need of a national revolution. She had long since achieved her unity, and her centralized power apparatus remained through one regime after another. In Germany both social equality and national consolidation were still to be achieved, with endless pains. And the need of the nation for unity and power was just as elemental and as deeply rooted in history as was the cry for domestic freedom and equality arising from those classes which the authoritarian state had so far kept down. Dahlmann in Frankfurt even voiced the opinion that within the German desire for both power and freedom, the stronger impulse was now directed toward power, which had thus far been denied. The criminal excesses reached in our day by the need for power in Germany should by no means mislead us into condemning the elemental national craving of the men of '48. For theirs was a genuine hunger for something indispensable. Even Goethe had once acknowledged this fact, after the battle of Leipzig. "Art and science," he said to Luden, "are universal, and in view of these the bonds of nationality disappear. But the consolation they afford is but hollow comfort, and cannot replace the proud consciousness of belonging to a great, strong, feared and respected nation." Basically all the cravings of the year 1848 were permeated by kindred feelings and experiences. There was a general desire to leave behind the constricting and now intolerable bonds of the past, as one leaves behind a dark and airless dungeon. Just as the little man felt himself generally neglected and mistreated by the authoritarian state, so did the more cultivated German, who saw himself as a member of a great national community, and yet hemmed in by the irritating boundaries and the often ridiculous parochialism of thirty-eight greater or smaller authoritarian states. And equally neglected and thrust aside did he feel himself and his whole people to be within the entire body of European states.

All three of these desires (the liberal, the national, the European) were now, it was fondly hoped, to find their fulfilment through the Frankfurt National Assembly which, elected by universal and equal suffrage, convened on the 18th of May. Let us consider its social composition; it was noticeably different from what one might have expected as the result of the democratic suffrage imported from France. It contained no workers, only one genuine peasant, few members of the lower middle class, but many lawyers and judges—and, as is well known, many professors; nor were representatives of business and industry lacking. This indicates the still remaining respect of the lower for the upper strata of society, especially for the academically educated and in general for what is termed the upper bourgeoisie. But the same masses who now cast their votes for these people, were simultaneously in a state of unruly and turbulent commotion, which must necessarily have boded evil for the upper middle class interests and ideals. One had to rely on such an energetic thrust from below, in order to succeed at all to Frankfurt and the Paulskirche. But now it was a question, indeed, whether one could continue to employ these energies as indispensable weapons against the rulers, and yet keep them within limits, so as to guard against anarchy and the overturn of the social order.

In the last analysis, it was the danger of communism which appeared to threaten the whole bourgeoisie—not only the upper but the lower middle class as well. How real even the latter felt this threat to be, is exemplified by the bloody clash between the civil guard and the workers in Berlin on October 16, 1848. Communistic slogans and demands rang out from the enraged masses. A clearly conceived program, such as that of Marx and Engels, was in truth limited at first to the narrowest circles. But in a broader perspective, it appears that the very existence of a communist movement was perhaps decisive, or at least instrumental, in determining the course of events in 1848—and, in the first instance, the attitude and policy of the Paulskirche. For it was in view of this communist threat that the middle class and its representation in the majority parties of the Paulskirche again and again were forced over toward the Right, toward some kind of compromise with the old authorities and their military resources. The same threat was instrumental in preventing the maintenance of a unified revolutionary purpose within the whole people, to which perhaps the government might at last have been forced to submit. We use the little word "perhaps," because historical questions of this sort cannot be treated like a mere problem in mathematics; because in every case where we have to consider the historical possibility of another kind of development than that which actually took place, an unknown "X" disturbs the calculation.

In any event, the parties of the majority—right and left center—which desired to establish a liberal, constitutional nation-state with an hereditary Prussian emperor as its head, found themselves in an extremely contradictory and precarious position. They needed the resources of a revolution just as much as those of a counter-revolution. But their position did not enable them to make full and unqualified use of either, without endangering the very basis of their undertaking. In their effort, however, to pursue a middle course and to bring both revolutionary and counter-revolutionary resources simultaneously or alternately into play, they incurred the danger, in turn, of becoming powerless themselves, and of seeing their cause wrecked against the forces of the stronger contender of the two—the counter-revolution. This, viewed as a whole, was to be their fate. Let us briefly point out here only the critical stages.

From France the signal had been given in February for the revolution; from France again the signal was given for the counter-revolution in June. In a terrible, three-day street battle, Cavaignac smashed the Paris workers. To be sure, the German middle class heaved a sigh of relief; but for them the ebbing of the revolutionary wave which now followed in Germany as well, was gain and loss alike—while for the reactionary forces of the authoritarian state, this turn constituted a clear gain. With the decline of communist fortunes, those of national liberalism sank as well.

This same dynamic course of events then unfolded during September. When the Prussian government concluded with Denmark the truce of Malmö, which seriously threatened the German claim to Schleswig, the aroused majority in the Paulskirche at first rejected it outright; but shortly thereafter, in view of the impracticable consequences of a refusal, the assembly, once more grown meek, ratified the agreement. And when an uprising from the Left now led to street fighting in Frankfurt itself and endangered the assembly, it was forced to turn for help to Prussian and Austrian troops (from the federal fortress at Mainz), in order to prevent a general landslide to the Left. Once more the fortunes of the authoritarian state rose, once more those of national liberalism sank. And they dropped still lower when the governments of Austria and Prussia, in October and November respectively, put down with their own military forces the rebellious democracy in Vienna and Berlin.

Under such circumstances was born the constitutional project of the Frankfurt National Assembly, culminating in the choice of the King of Prussia as hereditary emperor on March 28, 1849. Doubtless it was a proud achievement of the noblest aspiration toward national unity and freedom. But it lacked the basis of power which would have been necessary to put it through against the particularistic and reactionary forces of the authoritarian state. It was defeated at once when Frederick William IV, on April 3, 1849, refused to accept the new crown offered to him—a crown which in his view could appear only as a product of the revolution, a Danaean gift. And when the genuine revolution now reared its head again, and the disappointment which broad masses of the people experienced over the failure of Frankfurt exploded in the May uprisings in the Pfalz and Baden, the equally disillusioned middle class—in order not to be engulfed altogether by revolution and the social upheaval that might follow—was forced once more, as in September, 1848, to lean on the authoritarian state. It had now exhausted its own role as an independent power factor, and had to be satisfied with the scant dole of liberal and national concessions which the insight of those who ruled Prussia might still be willing to grant. The May uprisings, on the other hand, were easily put down by Prussian troops. The fighters of the revolution, be they idealists of the urban educated class, little people of the lower bourgeoisie, or workers, proved completely inadequate to wage a military campaign against the disciplined and dependable fighting force of the authoritarian state.

Upon these rocks was wrecked the German revolution. Only a unified revolutionary purpose, reconciling workers with bourgeoisie and upper with lower middle class, might have been able (as we have noted) to force another result and so to weaken the army's tradition of loyalty as to overthrow the old authorities. But the social transformation of the people, which brought on disruption within the entire middle class, had in fact made impossible from the first the growth of such a spirit of revolutionary unity. Without this social transformation, however—without a rising upper middle class, a lower middle class threatened with disintegration, and an aspiring working class—the revolution itself would have been impossible. Thus strangely and tragically intertwined were the inner necessity of this revolution and its inevitable failure.

Born and educated in Switzerland, ROBERT
SAITSCHICK (1868–1965) was for many years a
professor at the University of Cologne. He is the
author of thirty-four books, most of them in the fields
of literature, religion, and philosophy. His only
work on German political history is a study of
Bismarck published late in his career. It contains a
chapter entitled "Bismarck's Machiavellianism" from
which this selection is taken. The characteristics
Saitschick saw in Bismarck were those that won him the
sobriquet "Iron Chancellor."*

Man of Blood and Iron

The destruction of the German Confederation could only have fateful consequences. This creation of the Congress
of Vienna was, despite its inadequacy,
the last expression of the German political tradition. Its constitution guaranteed
the inviolability and independence of
the individual German states, which
pledged not to engage in war against
one another under any pretext and
agreed to settle their disputes without
violence. The international character of
the constitution anticipated future developments. It gave the central European states five decades of uninterrupted
peace, and it even sheltered Prussia, the
border state, which had gradually built
for itself a special position. At least this

was true as long as Prussia, like Austria,
consciously belonged to that body.

Bismarck must have intended from the
beginning to destroy the German Confederation in order to end the rivalry
between Austria and Prussia. His sentiments were entirely Prussian. In his
speech to the North German Reichstag
on March 11, 1867, after he had come
close to his goal by excluding Austria
from Germany, he spoke contemptuously of the "comfortable attitudes to
which we became accustomed in Germany during a half century of peace."
Such a peace was repugnant to him. He
paid no attention to the roots from
which the German Confederation had
sprung. It had grown out of the wars of

* From Robert Saitschick, *Bismarck und das Schicksal des deutschen Volkes* (Munich: Ernst
Reinhardt Verlag, 1949), omitting the original footnotes. Translated by Otto Pflanze. By permission of Ernst Reinhardt Verlag.

liberation, as the antithesis of Napoleon's conquering centralization, and had established an equilibrium between the large and small states for the protection of international law. This was its moral basis.

To Bismarck's contemporaries, who retained an instinctive feeling for the German character, his politics seemed like a revival of Bonapartism. This opinion was often uttered by the Welfs and Catholics but also by Germans throughout the south. A number of thoughtful men could not escape the conclusion that the "civil war" of 1866 was wicked and that the political ideas to which Bismarck subscribed were utterly alien to the German character. They were, furthermore, in contradiction to everything that Bismarck himself had earlier stood for in the Prussian Landtag and Erfurt parliament. In November 1850 he had worked for the meeting between Otto von Manteuffel and Prince Felix zu Schwarzenberg at Olmütz and had described Austria as a German state and an indispensable member of the German Confederation. Did this represent his actual conviction at that time or did it stem from ulterior motive? Was it his purpose to gain the favor of Frederick William IV through Leopold von Gerlach and by this means secure his own appointment to the Confederate diet at Frankfurt? Or can we assume that Bismarck underwent a fundamental change in outlook? The refusal of Frederick William IV to accept the crown offered to him by the majority in the Frankfurt National Assembly in 1848 [sic] was at any rate in accord with the political outlook of Bismarck, for the combination of "freedom and unity" was certainly repugnant to him.

[Soon after his appointment to the Frankfurt diet in 1851] Bismarck's thought and actions came into conflict with the conviction he had only recently expressed concerning the sanctity of historic rights. He had said that he wished to see the Prussian eagle free, neither bound by a new imperial diet like that which had convened in Regensburg nor clipped by the egalitarian shears of the Frankfurt parliament. "Prussian we are and Prussian we wish to remain," he had cried out in his Landtag speech of October 6, 1849. In one of his letters to Leopold von Gerlach in 1853 he wrote, "We would come out better with the other confederate states if we took a generally bolder and freer attitude toward them, without clothing our policy, which is actually Prussian and egoistic, in the mangy ermine of German patriotism. They aren't fooled by that; they detect the purpose." And immediately after that he wrote, "We must not let ourselves be entangled in either our own or in alien phrases about 'German policy,' but must boldly proclaim a specifically Prussian policy." And four years later he spoke of a "specific Prussian patriotism," to which he "subordinates everything else." His political outlook was a mixture of Prussianism and Bonapartism. When General Leopold von Gerlach reproached him for paying homage to Bonapartism, he answered "Bonapartism is older among us Prussians, I would like to assert, than Bonaparte." In June 1865 he said to the Italian minister Govone, "I am much less German than Prussian and would have no qualms about agreeing to cede to France the entire region between the banks of the Rhine and the Mosel." The words "Red reactionary, who reeks of blood" with which Frederick William IV described Bismarck in the year 1849, fittingly characterize this great man of violence (*Gewaltmensch*), to whom all that mattered was the calculated end and who had no scruples in his choice of means. This loyal vassal of the king had already spoken in the early 1860s of "the sovereignty swindle of the German princes." While Richelieu said that he had no enemies other than those of the king, Bismarck could have said that he had no friends other than those who forwarded his own plans—plans that he pursued with diplomatic skill and at the same time with Machiavellian recklessness. August Bebel remarked that Bismarck would have allied himself with the devil and the devil's grandmother if he could have thereby gained an advantage. That remark brilliantly describes the Machiavellism of Bismarck.

Bismarck began to pursue his "criminal sport with the most holy things" (as Crown Prince Frederick remarked about Bismarck's foreign policy) with all his usual energy. The German Confederation was not to be rebuilt on a new and sounder foundation; it was to be destroyed from the ground up. Prussian historians, obsessed as they were by nationalism, were not justified in portraying the German Confederation in a distorted light. The peace treaty of Westphalia and that of 1815, which still held the whole of Western culture within its horizon, were undermined by a policy that was nothing else but barbarism in disguise. There could no longer be any talk of a community of European peoples and states; instead of being bound together, peoples were systematically separated from one another. Strangely enough, liberalism, immediately upon being united with nationalism, contributed the most to the disruption of the European community. This meant the forced continuation of the process of centralization begun under Napoleon. While the German Confederation was based on peaceful aims, the outcome of the new politics could only be war and the destruction of the European community. Hence one can understand the cry of Cardinal Antonelli, "Europe does not exist any more."

The year 1866 with its epilogue in 1870 was the fateful turning point for the Western community of nations. An unrestrained nationalism came to occupy the foreground of European politics and recklessly began to exert its influence everywhere. The respect for treaties practically disappeared from political life. The glorification of power found its ultimate expression in naked Machiavellism and in the pseudo-biological theories of political naturalism.

ARNOLD O. MEYER (1877–1944) was a lifelong
researcher on Bismarck. Monographs on Bismarck's
religious life and early diplomatic career at
Frankfurt during the 1850s prepared Meyer for
his greatest undertaking, a biography from which this
selection is taken. The book was finished during
World War II and some reviewers have seen in its
praise of Bismarck a veiled criticism of Hitler.
Meyer's interpretation is representative of the school
of German historical writing that continues to regard
Bismarck as a German rather than a Prussian
patriot. "The national idea," Meyer writes,
"was his lodestar."*

Great National Hero

Although our great statesman often had to swim against the current of the times, Bismarck was, in his devotion to the national idea, entirely a man of his age. Yet he recognized the impossiblity of creating a purely national state. Concern for the security of the state did not permit him to consider granting the Polish subjects of the king of Prussia autonomous rights merely to exclude an alien body from the nation. For the same reason he had to take Danish and later French minorities—albeit reluctantly— under the German roof. On the other hand his great task required that he exclude the Austrian Germans. At the time there was no other way to abolish the old evil of German discord and to erect a strong Reich in place of a loose confederation in which no truly national development, no union of popular strength, was possible.

The exclusion of Austria was more than the defeat of German dualism. It was also a salutary breach with a past that could no longer survive and yet did not want to die. A nonpartisan observer such as Sir Robert Morier, who, through diplomatic service in Frankfurt and Vienna, was acquainted equally well with conditions in Austria and the German Confederation, condemned Bismarck's methods, to be sure, but approved of his ends. Morier expressed the conviction that "the complete victory of Austria in this war, and the recovery of

* From A. O. Meyer, *Bismarck, Der Mensch und der Staatsmann* (Stuttgart: K. F. Koehler Verlag, 1949), pp. 334–337, translated by Dennis Showalter and Otto Pflanze. By permission of K. F. Koehler Verlag.

her prestige in Italy and Germany, would be the greatest misfortune that could happen to Europe, generally, and to Germany, Italy, and *Austria* in particular." Austria could never be united with Germany but Prussia might. For Germany, therefore, every Prussian success was a gain, every Austrian success a loss. And Austria itself could flourish only by parting with Germany.

Austria had a supranational structure in the age of the national state and was the obstacle to the national development of central Europe. The old German Empire, from which Austria had inherited its tradition and dignity, had also been supranational. The political thinking of our people showed supranational characteristics. Deep in the German consciousness lies a tendency to set the general above the particular; to strive and struggle under the banner of a universal ethical ideal. Germans have been moved by several conceptions of this kind: religious faiths and ecclesiastical ideals; the doctrine of the unity of mankind and humanistic ideals of education, and political systems based on ideas of human dignity, religion, or morality. All of them had in common a nonpolitical *(ausserstaatlich)* and supranational character which governed the attitudes of the Germans toward their state and fatherland. This was especially true toward the end of the eighteenth and the beginning of the nineteenth centuries, when national consciousness was tinged with cosmopolitanism. The intellectual influence of this age extended to the early years of Bismarck. Ludwig von Gerlach[1] indeed

extolled as a noble characteristic of the German people their inability to submit themselves to a narrow-minded national consciousness, their capacity to rise above their own egos to higher ideals. He was proud that German history had never been motivated by "the mere idea of the size, unity, and power of the nation." In the Middle Ages, it was centered on the Holy Roman Empire and the Church. In the sixteenth century, "the truth of God was more valuable to the German nation than national unity. They let unity disintegrate in the struggle over eternal truth." In the eighteenth century, literature was so much more important to the Germans than politics that they watched the collapse of their own political order with near indifference. As early as 1850, when he sat with Bismarck in the Erfurt parliament,[2] Gerlach warned that the establishment of nationality as the highest principle was a serious error that was doing much harm in political life. Authority established by the grace of God was the higher principle. He denounced Bismarck's policy of 1866 in the *Kreuzzeitung*:[3] "We must guard against that abhorrent heresy which teaches that God's holy commandments do not apply to the spheres of politics, diplomacy, and war and that these spheres have no higher law than patriotic egoism."

This great question—the relationship between politics and religion—ended the twenty-year friendship between Bismarck and Gerlach. After Gerlach had himself irreparably destroyed their political alliance by his attack in the *Kreuzzeitung*,

---

[1] Ludwig and Leopold von Gerlach were influential conservatives of the ultra, or "romantic," school. Ludwig was an important Prussian official and Leopold was a general in the Prussian army. The latter, who died in 1861, promoted the early career of Bismarck, while the former, who died in 1877, lived to witness the changes which their protégé wrought in Germany.—*Ed.*

[2] The Erfurt parliament was a German assembly summoned by Frederick William IV in 1850 to approve the "German Union" scheme launched by Radowitz. Bismarck and Ludwig von Gerlach were members of the opposition in the parliament.—*Ed.*

[3] The *Kreuzzeitung* was the principal newspaper of the conservative movement.—*Ed.*

"Uncle Ludwig," the old family friend, the godfather of Bismarck's oldest son, vainly asked the angry chancellor to continue at least their personal friendship. Bismarck answered the appeal "neither with word nor handclasp." In "that lacerating interview" (as Gerlach described it) on May 18, 1866, two men separated, but also two views of life, two distinct conceptions of God. For Gerlach, there was only the God of Scriptural revelation. For Bismarck, there was also the revelation of God in nature, which showed that conflict was the fundamental basis of all earthly existence, the creative order of the world.

The pacifist view of Christianity typical of a narrow orthodox faith was foreign to Bismarck's religious sentiment. Equally foreign to his political outlook was the subordination of the national idea to those supranational values, the high esteem for which Gerlach believed to be a special virtue of the Germans. Certainly devotion to these lofty ideals had always contributed much to formation of the German personality. In politics, however, such an outlook must lead to a denial of the national state. Furthermore, the priority given to general principles over practical politics led easily to the elevation of party ideals above the welfare of the state. This was as true for the liberals, with their goal of popular sovereignty and parliamentary government, as for the conservatives, with their dogmas of legitimacy. Bismarck differed from the overwhelming majority of his countrymen in that he nowhere acknowledged principles, neither in domestic, foreign, nor economic affairs. No heaven other than that of state and fatherland arched above his political world. The only standard by which he judged any party was its momentary utility for the attainment of his highest goal: "to make the Germans

into a nation." He found the best means for accomplishing this in the old Prussia of Frederick the Great. Yet here too Bismarck acknowledged no principle and no idea other than the supreme majesty of the state. He had to hammer Prussian iron into the too-soft metal of the German political consciousness.

The German Confederation was not a national structure. Its creators intended it to serve supranational at least as much as national ends. "One must never forget," wrote Wilhelm von Humboldt in 1816, "the true and actual purpose of the Confederation in its connection with European politics. This purpose is to secure the peace." If extended too far, the concept of unity, Humboldt thought, would give the Confederation a false direction; it could divert the Confederation from its role as the guardian of peace to the path of conquest, something "which no true German can desire." This attitude remained alive—along with the striving for national unity, through Bismarck's time and beyond, in so far as the rejection of conquest was concerned. The deposed elector of Hesse found a clever propagandist who sought to prove that the dissolution of the German Confederation was a misfortune for Europe and a curse for Germany: "Only the free, federal union of the German peoples, and not the deceitful gift from Prussia of a Reich united by force" would provide a Germany capable of guaranteeing the general tranquility and security and of preserving the peace of the entire continent as well as of Germany itself. Unitary and militarily organized states have a warlike, disruptive character, while federations, being limited by their nature and constitution to mutual defense, are incapable of attack. This opinion is similar to that held by Humboldt and yet it is an error of political thought that history has long refuted. To a country with open frontiers such as Germany, the inability to attack meant the inability to defend. Therefore the tranquility of Europe was endangered rather than guaranteed by Germany's federative organization. The Thirty Years' War and the aggressive wars of Louis XIV and Napoleon were possible only because of the weakness of a federated central Europe.

Bismarck's policy meant the renunciation of these supranational ideas, and the year 1866 marked the most decisive turning point in the development of the political outlook of the German people. The prosperity and dignity of the nation was the single goal of German unification, not service to Europe. No European shackles, no rights of intervention by foreign powers, should in the future limit the free self-determination of the Germans. Through this policy Germany has become great, and Europe has not been the worse for it. Since the completion of German unification the guarantee of peace in Europe has depended on the strength of its center, and the period of peace lasted longer under the shield of the Bismarckian Reich than under any other before or since.

Thus the shortest war of our history brought about the greatest changes and ushered in a new age. The fruit of the war was not the deepening but the overcoming of conflicts within Germany, not division but unity and strength. And the miracle in which no one had believed happened: the German question was settled without a hostile neighbor's setting foot on German soil.

In 1936 HANS ROTHFELS (1891–   ), then a
professor at the University of Königsberg, left
Germany to teach at Brown University and
the University of Chicago. He returned to Germany
in 1951, ending his career at the University of
Tübingen. In several monographs and articles he has
dealt with aspects of Bismarck's statesmanship and
the characteristics of nationalism. This selection is
from an essay that introduces a volume of
documents illustrative of Bismarck's political outlook.
Here Rothfels makes a final assessment of the
subject that has been his greatest interest as a scholar.*

Responsible Statesman

Today scarcely anyone seriously doubts
that a deep gulf separates all that the
Führer of the Third Reich thought and
did from Bismarck's politics and the
views that his politics expressed. Recently
Theodor Heuss[1] characterized the old
chancellor correctly as a man "who was
very wise, very cultured, and very sober,
and who, with all his daring, imagina-
tion and boldness of method knew himself to be under the law of moderation."
Indeed, the appropriation [of Bismarck]
as a "forerunner" [of Hitler] by National
Socialist propaganda has faded away, as
has   the   counterpropaganda,   which
joined together the most varied elements
indiscriminately. Reading the documents
printed here may be useful in dealing
with the aftereffects of such distortions.
They make exceedingly clear what never
should have been doubted: that Bismarck proceeded in his thought and action from the state or, more precisely,
from Prussia, but in any case not from
the nation, let alone the race. They show
instead that the passions of popular nationalism   and   uninhibited   biological
forces constituted for him an important
source of danger for the existence of
Germany and Europe. In his opinion
even nationality (*Volkstum*) was basically
something chaotic which could play a
historical role only through the state.

[1] Theodor Heuss, German professor, historian, and first president (1949–1959) of the German Federal Republic.—*Ed.*

---

* From Hans Rothfels, *Bismarck und der Staat*, 2d ed. (Stuttgart: Wissenschaftliche Buchgesellschaft, 1954), pp. xvii–xxviii, translated by Herbert Levine. By permission of the author and
the Wissenschaftliche Buchgesellschaft.

Yet did he not himself look upon the state as mere driving force, as nothing else but power which, especially in the case of the "large state," had "its only sound basis" in egoism and hence was not limited by principles and ideas? And did he not, in a very personal way, translate into practice this view of the large state as elevated above the sphere of value relationships and postulates? While acting with technical virtuosity and with great insight and inventiveness, did he not always concentrate on the concept of power? Can we speak of a philosophy of the state (*Staatsanschauung*) in a definite sense, or even of its incorporation into an international context, in a man who was contemptuous of all idealistic programs, a man who stated with disdain that the word "Europe" was always to be found in the mouths of those politicians "who desired from other powers that which they didn't dare to demand in their own name"? Can this "skeptical realist," as he is often conceived to have been, be placed in any context at all?

Indeed, Bismarck is generally seen (and rightly so) as the great empiricist who, totally unprejudiced by theories, exploited political forces wherever they appeared, allying himself first with one power then with another. Unlimited by dogmas in domestic as in foreign affairs, he changed fronts repeatedly and unexpectedly in the struggles over the foundation and internal development of the Empire. No party could, nor can, call him entirely its own, but at the same time he was not so far removed from any of the parties that he could not invade the realm of their ideas and appropriate parts of their programs. All these elements are found simultaneously and successively in the image of Bismarck's political character: extreme Junkerism and alliance with the forces of revolution, aristocratic rebellion and ministerial absolutism, divine right and *raison d'état*, nationalist politics and a rejection of all irredentism, Manchester liberalism and state socialism, belief in military force and conflict with it, Prussian militarism and the primacy of civil authority, struggle against democracy and a later appeal to parliamentarianism.

It appears to be only a step from this statement to the reproach that he lacked political character or that he exercised a power of demagogic seduction that robbed other men, or even an entire people, of their "character" and of the courage of their convictions; and hence that he at least sowed the seeds for acceptance of an authoritarian regime. Criticisms of this kind cannot be simply disregarded, no matter how many links in the alleged chain of causality they leave out. It is not our purpose to make either harmless or harmonious a man who well knew how to combine successfully reckless disclosure with diplomatic subtlety, who was capable of hating in a elemental way and who himself confessed that there were hidden recesses in his soul into which he let no one look. In the heat of the struggle he bent characters and expended talents, seemingly following a purely utilitarian ethic. The *clausula rebus sic stantibus*, which his memoirs propagated as his legacy, seems to dissolve everything solid. It has been aptly said that the concept of power built into the new Empire kept those forces that were ready to share responsibility in the "antechamber of power" and "denatured" them. Certainly Bismarck helped in his way to liquidate the ideological content of the older German parties. The liberal opposition was for the most part converted to *Realpolitik* and subjected to the corroding law of success. Through him the conservatives were diverted away from their lofty principles and toward the pursuit of their material interests. It can even be said (and, in a certain sense, with regret) that those two parties which were the most strongly principled and with which he collided the most severely—namely, the Center and Social Democratic parties—were sooner or later re-educated by his influence to opportunism and revisionism. It can also be said, moreover, that the Kulturkampf and the antisocialist law created wounds that healed only with difficulty, or alienated whole sections of the people. No one would wish to overlook this. It is also true that after hard experience we have become alert to the danger to which the dignity of the individual, the majesty of law, and universal principles are exposed by the concept of state power and by the concentration of political authority. Erich Eyck, in his biography of Bismarck written in England during World War II, says with good reason that this danger was the heaviest mortgage that Bismarck laid upon the structure of the Empire. It arose from the very skill with which he grasped and employed without reserve every means to gain his ends. Eyck concluded that Bismarck, despite great political gifts, lacked a sense of justice. Another judgment frequently heard today is that the decisive weakness of his work was the lack of a binding ideal, the absense of any connection with a universal order.

Obviously, two questions remain unanswered here. First, there is the problem of whether the trend toward realism and empiricism, which was a characteristic of the post-March [1848] period of the nineteenth century in all areas of life, can be attributed essentially to a single individual; whether instead Bismarck did not place definite limits on the growth of natural forces, and whether his conception of the state, his "étatism," did not provide a moderating and ordering principle that contained them. We will return to this question. For the moment another is more important: whether Bismarck was in fact so unlimited and sovereign, so "free" in the use of every means, as his actions and words would at first make it seem. There is no doubt that he himself gave the initial impetus to this interpretation. He once said, "If I were to go through life with principles, I would feel as though I had to walk a narrow path in the forest and had to carry a long stick in my mouth." There is no doubt about the pertinence of this metaphor and the political attitude it describes. Hence it could be easy, and has been easy, to conclude that the only principle in Bismarck's politics was to have no principles at all. We can surely say that the essence of Bismarck's political conception was the freedom from all system, the recognition of what "is" and the demands that this imposes rather than the pursuit of what "ought to be," of what is alien to reality. In fact, it was this attitude that separated him, the Junker from the Altmark,[2] from his conservative friends and social peers and gave him a distinct voice. The proper function of diplomacy in his view was not to engage in the struggle for realization of constitutional and religious-ethical ideals but to seek the welfare of one's own state. When he was the youthful representative [of Prussia] at the diet of the German Confederation, he wrote to Leopold von Gerlach, moderating his words rather deliberately in

[2] Altmark was a district in central Prussia in which Schönhausen, the ancestral seat of the Bismarck family, was located.—*Ed.*

view of the reproachful attitude of his friend, "I am Prussian, and my ideal in foreign policy is to be free of prejudice so as to be able to make decisions without being influenced by feelings of dislike or love for foreign states and their rulers." Just as Bismarck, though a monarchist, breached the principle of legitimacy, he also broke the international law of the *status quo* and the domestic law of the constitution if it appeared to him to be a question of the vital interests and the autonomy of Prussia.

Nevertheless, it cannot be concluded that his concept of the state lacked a challenging impetus or that his politics lacked entirely an element of universal order. They were merely based upon another "principle," as the letter to Gerlach most clearly shows. Just as it would be unjustified to dogmatize from any details of his actions, it would clearly be wrong to make a dogma out of his fundamental inclination to be undogmatic and to present his attitude as unrestricted. In other words, Bismarck's realism—attained through struggle, containing inner tensions of which he was aware, and responsive to the countermoves of other forces—is not to be confused with the soulless, professional opportunism into which the conception of Bismarck held by his successors degenerated. Certainly, making a theory out of untheoretical politics could easily lead to a mere worship of success or to a conception of the "art of the possible" as the "merely" possible. In the former lay the tendency toward an apotheosis of power, in the latter that toward the line of least resistance—the diagonal and the zigzag. A "misunderstood Bismarck" could be, and has been, conjured up to justify the one as well as the other. In view of this it appears all the more valid and impor-

tant, for a clearer understanding of his conception of the state and of the "internal structure" of his politics, to reconstruct at least an accurate historical picture of the relationship in his mind between freedom and obligation, conviction and deed, idea and power.

To be sure, this requires a correct reading of Bismarck's own statements, carried through without unjustifiably isolating them from their context. Many of his pointed words had a polemical meaning. Even the statement about following a narrow path through the forest with stick in mouth was clearly directed against one front, against what might be called the German inclination toward hobbyhorse politics. In addition, its actual point was not the assertion of a sovereign freedom of choice but of the limitations imposed upon that freedom by the "narrowness" of the path, leaving out of account such other limiting factors as his relationship to the king. In a similarly fundamental way Bismarck spoke of the politics of a great state as having to follow "definite tracks." On another occasion he gave the metaphor of the forest a twist that perhaps best describes his view that firmness of principle must be combined with flexibility of tactics. In a conversation with the Austrian historian Friedjung, he compared the statesman with a "wanderer in the woods who knows in what general direction he is going, but not at what point he will emerge from the forest."

It is not accidental, and it is interesting in several ways for our theme, that the image of the forest appears so frequently in Bismarck's thought. It is well known that he came from the countryside, politically from the aristocratic tradition of self-administration. To an important degree this gave a social color to his politics, which were by no means rootless and undiscriminating, and even more so to his basic conception of political and social life. The "conserving air" which he saw in the provincial patriarchy, in the longevity and family loyalty of the household servants, he saw also in the forest, which continually renews itself and yet remains the same. By nature he was, so to speak, closer to the growing than to the making, and all his life he sought to draw refreshment from nature and its power of renovation. "When I sleep well," he said on occasion, "I dream of fir nurseries that stand fresh and green in the spring and, damp from the rain, send out long shoots. Then I wake up totally refreshed." He was in the habit of expressing his own feeling for growing things with the motto that he once read over the gate of a forestry school, "We reap what we have not sown, and sow what we will not reap." He could not have characterized more strikingly his conviction that politics must be anchored in the perpetual and that the statesman is limited in his actions by the continuity of life.

It is necessary to pursue this theme a little further, certainly not for the purpose of remaking Bismarck into a quietist or into a mere executive agent of forces external to himself, but in order to make apparent the tension inherent in his concept of the state and his alledgedly unlimited realism. There is no doubt that he was drawn to the state by his personal will to achieve and by his awareness of his own powers. "I want to make music as it sounds good to me or none at all." The prospect of being a "statesman under a free constitution," of being a "participant in energetic movements," attracted him like a magnet, just as he never denied his sympathy for English social and political institutions. However, he first learned to know

the state in the arid form of the pre-March administration, the "Prussian state in nightshirt and slippers," as it has been aptly said. The impressions that he received then [as an apprentice civil servant] sent him, horrified, back into the isolation of the countryside and continued to influence him all his life. He entered politics not as an official but as an opposition deputy of the most extreme right during the revolutionary period. He was full of mistrust for rootless individuals, "men without an acre of land." He was never free from an inclination to retreat back "under the cannons of Schönhausen," or from pride in the fact that the Bismarcks had been residents in the district of the Mark before the Hohenzollerns. Even as a minister he saw the state simultaneously from above and from below, both as a man of social independence and as a part of the *contribuens plebs*. In 1869 he complained of the "lack of independence in a people that has been accustomed for centuries to let the government alone take care of them." This letter, which has been only recently discovered, rings genuine, although its wording does show some tactical consideration for the liberal minister and colleague to whom it was sent. Since the days of Baron vom Stein,[3] no German statesman had said such harsh things about bureaucracy in government: about the "boa constrictor" of the civil service; about the bureaucratic apparatus that spread "like subsoil water" and whose "legal excrements" were the "most natural filth" in the world. He felt the bureaucracy to be "liberal" because it believed in "making" things. And yet, being a statesman of

[3] Baron Friedrich vom und zum Stein, Prussian minister (1807–1808) and principal architect of the Prussian reforms of the Napoleonic period.—*Ed.*

elemental force, he himself interfered in the fate of the world and altered it. For three decades he not only ruled, but administrated in the most vigorous way, and under him the bureaucracy carried out essential parts of the work of political and social reform.

This paradoxical tension will always be found at the heart of Bismarck's view of the state. Considering everything, it is debatable whether he should be called a Junker. However, if this term, which is so often misunderstood (being incorrectly associated with nationalism and imperialism) is to be applied to him, it must be used in the sense of aloofness from the government apparatus; of the mistrust, never completely overcome, of a "vassal from the Mark" for the absolute state (*Racker Staat*). We may say that Bismarck was and remained enough of a Junker so that he could never be what we today call a "totalitarian." In spite of this, he came to see himself as a man of the state, and public affairs seized him to such a degree that he could complain in his old age that "politics has killed all the other fish in my carp pond."

This contradiction cannot be resolved by referring to Bismarck's willful nature and his personal ambition. While he inflated the Prussian-Frederician tradition with his own passions, his fighting spirit and his excitable sense of honor, he simultaneously joined his own being to a state personality that was the product of historical growth. The tasks that he assumed were in existence before him and without him. He did not create them, he merely took them over. Again we must remember Bismarck's sense for the organic and the unplanned and his figures of speech, which had more than a mere literary significance. By preference he took them from the life of the

hunter and angler, who [as he expressed it] must know how to wait, who first tests and feels out the ground before he takes his next step. He saw in this a similarity to the activity of the statesman, not only insofar as the capacity to feel out tactical situations was concerned, but also in establishing the interconnection between past and present in the developing life of the state. Here Bismarck stood upon a basic conviction that first made political action meaningful to him, especially in the domestic sphere (which he did not at all regard as merely a reflection of external power relationships). He expressed this train of thought in 1882, in what was for him an unusually theoretical and pointed, almost sententious, form. At that time the question was raised whether the burden of accident insurance should be imposed partially on the existing generation for the benefit of future generations. Taking the affirmative position, the chancellor wrote to Bötticher,[4] "The passing of individuals is irrelevant. . . . The state and its institutions are only possible if they are thought of as personalities with permanent identities."

Bismarck's view of the state as an organism is reminiscent of romantic political philosophy. But the same kind of observation concerning constancy in the midst of change could be made by Anglo-Saxons, to whom romanticization of the state is completely alien. Where party governments and leaders alternate in power, the "permanent identity," even though differently conceived, finds its expression in the effectiveness of politicians in the grand manner. It is not far fetched to compare Roosevelt's New

[4] Karl Heinrich von Bötticher, German vice chancellor, Reich state secretary of the interior, and Prussian minister, who was one of Bismarck's collaborators in designing the German social insurance legislation of the 1880s.—*Ed.*

Deal with Bismarck's social insurance legislation from this point of view (as well as others). The point, at any rate, is that in the case of the first chancellor of the Reich this conception established a basis for the greatest personal determination. It gave him the conviction that he was, if not the "organ," then the "servant" of a transcendental being. It was the consciousness of this connection that first really released his capacity for energetic action. Despite considerable tension, in fact, the contradiction between Bismarck's tendency toward personal domination and his attitude of *inserviendo consumor* is not beyond resolution. The many, most surprising changes of course that Bismarck executed do not defy (or make a mere phrase of) *fert unda nec regitur*, which Bismarck wrote as a campaign motto in a journal during the war of 1870–1871. The feeling of being "carried along" was a basic element in his conception of political life. We do not have to invoke psychoanalysis (as has been done) to be aware of the role of the unconscious in such a sober realist. He himself said that his best decisions were made by the "other fellow" in him; it was as though the scale, after fluctuating for a long time, suddenly stood still when a spring snapped into place. This also refutes, albeit from a new angle, the view that he was subject to arbitrary whims. Repeatedly Bismarck expressed the conviction that the history of the nation is a "broad stream" whose course no individual, not even the ruler, can direct: "World history as a whole cannot possibly be made." "Man," he acknowledged in his old age, "cannot create the stream of time, but only float and steer upon it."

Such words were not inspired by a wisdom derived from reflection and a sense of resignation and certainly not by purposeful modesty. To steer was in itself a task of the highest order. Although Bismarck has been critized for acting "against the ideas of the time," it should be asked whether, in many respects, he did not rather yield to them too much. We will come back to this when we discuss the content of his politics and their conceptual side. For the moment we are concerned with form rather than content and with the relationship between freedom and containment as it underlay Bismarck's view of the state. More than once and in various versions he expressed his basic feeling that the statesman can do nothing better than listen carefully for the rustle of "God's cloak," as it moves through human events, and seek to snatch at the hem.

This raises the question of the *religious* element in Bismarck's view of the state. This too is a controversial subject, for into it has been injected [the accusation that his religious attitude was influenced by] considerations of utility and social respectability, by a kind of familial and class "mimicry," and even in some degree by the primacy of foreign policy. When Bismarck's youthful crisis was resolved by a conversion to a personal God, he simultaneously won a bride, a "valuable" outlook on the world, and a connection with the Pietist circle in Pomerania that had previously eyed the titanic Junker with concern. The famous suitor's letter to Herr von Puttkamer[5] is usually seen as the first masterpiece of a diplomatic virtuoso and, on the tactical plane, this is certainly correct. Through his conversion Bismarck first achieved

[5] Heinrich von Puttkamer, the father of Bismarck's future wife, Johanna von Puttkamer, and a member of the Pietist movement within the Lutheran church.—*Ed.*

an "alliance capability" (*Bündnisfähig-keit*), which was also to become a primary goal of his foreign policy. His letters to his fiancée and wife show that he was well aware of the kind of world to which he was speaking. Yet all this should not mislead one into denying the genuine religious content of the event of his conversion or into misunderstanding it as an attempt by this man of genius to "take out insurance." The most notable thing about it was the genuine submission of an arbitrary and self-destructive will. It was a spontaneous not a purposeful act which found liberation in prayer and which lasted beyond the immediate situation that produced it and endured throughout his life. It is well known what the *Loosungen und Lehrtexte* of the Congregation of Brethren meant to Bismarck as a daily reference. He asked that a book of devotions and a psalter be sent to him during the war of 1870–1871. There is no doubt that he always felt himself responsible to God for his actions and believed that both state and statesman had a religious mission. To be sure, he asserted his belief in the Christian idea of the state and in the divine right of the Prussian monarchy in a more fiery and extreme fashion in his early speeches than was in harmony with the conceptions of a mature statesman who had outgrown the conflicts of the revolutionary era. Yet the basic view remained the same: the state and monarchy that he served were in their own ways part of the divine plan for the world, whose governance required that the rustle of the cloak be heard.

In addition, Bismarck's religious thinking colored in detail his views on domestic and foreign policy. It underlay his criticism of the "godless sovereignty swindle" of the German petty princes, as well as his rejection of any quest for prestige or of any departure from the vital interests of the state, soberly conceived, and especially his basic condemnation of preventive war, which presumed to force the hand of Providence. There is evidence, furthermore, that the social welfare activity of the state, which Bismarck advanced so decisively in certain directions, came from his "conscience," indeed, from his feeling for "human dignity." That it contained a Christian-patriarchal motive according to the Lutheran concept of authority is unmistakable, even if it was not that of "love." In fact, Bismarck's religious views even influenced his fighting position. To him, the social or socialist agitator was the "temptor" who promised heaven on earth. One of the important things which also separated him from liberal doctrine was the Lutheran belief in man's sinful nature. He believed neither in a harmoniously ordered world that needed only to be left to itself, nor in the harmonizing results of free competition. The doctrine of original sin prevented him from believing either. The world was worldly and full of evil. One could deal with it only through a sense of reality and worldly courage. The final strength lay in faith, in trust in God, and in the hope of forgiveness. Thus, in more than one respect religion was the "wonderful foundation" upon which Bismarck became a statesman. While limited by his convictions, he was, precisely because of the strength of his Lutheran faith, free in his political actions.

It is clear that Bismarck was always aware of the gulf between divine and earthly principles. From the very beginning his faith, aware of the world and pressing him to act, was far removed from that of his Pietist friends, although he too was not untouched by a feeling of *vanitas vanitatum*. Occasionally, and once right in the midst of a political crisis (1859), he remarked that "specific patriotism" paled in the face of the eternal. "As God wills, everything is but a question of time: nations and men, wisdom and folly, war and peace—they come and go like waves, and the sea remains. Before God what are our states and their power and honor other than anthills that are trampled by the hoof of an ox or beehives whose fate is determined by the peasant collecting honey. . ." At another time, almost thirty years later, he said, "We just do our duty in the present. God determines whether it will last." These are the overtones we cannot ignore in recognizing Bismarck's concept of the state, and we will meet them once more in connection with his anxous forebodings about the future. However, they receded into the background before his urge to act and his duty to cope with existing situations. Yet, it is true as a whole that Bismarck, because he found stability in his personal and religious life, won the strength to surmount the antinomies of the political profession without deifying the state or subjecting it directly to the commands of the Gospel.

This too is an attitude that lasted all his life, evident in his sober emphasis on the worldly and temporal laws of existence, as well as in his rejection of clerical politicians and "court theologians," including Stöcker.[6] He first expressed this memorable turn against politics based on principle and dogma (or crusading and revanchist politics, we would add today) in the letters he exchanged with Leopold von Gerlach in

---

[6] Adolf Stöcker, Prussian court preacher and founder of the anti-Semitic Christian-Social party.—*Ed.*

1857. Here he renounced the half natural-law, half Romantic-Christian dogmatism of his close friends who wished to bind the state to ideologies in the pursuit of its interests or to impose on it the yoke of their beliefs. He could have told them that they were actually irreligious egoists who valued their sympathies or antipathies and above all their own ease of conscience above the dutiful mastery of the tasks given to them by their vocations, thereby creating for themselves an "alibi" with which to meet reality. He saw the "embryo of disloyalty" to king and state in this self-righteousness, which he called, significantly enough, "personal arbitrariness." It was precisely his religious awe that gave him the strength to confront the reality of political life. Indeed he drew a feeling of superior morality from his unreserved recognition of the contradiction that existed between the lessons of the Sermon on the Mount and the demands of politics. He assured an anxious fellow conservative, "Whoever accuses me of being a man without conscience should first try his own conscience on this battlefield." It is simply not true that Bismarck possessed no convictions and no sense of justice, or that he banished morality from politics. His politics is more strongly permeated by it than is generally admitted. But he certainly held that in borderline cases he could not afford to follow his private opinions —at least, not without conflict—or even the demands of his private peace of conscience. This was an expression of responsibility in the face of great tasks and is indicative of a thoroughly religious conception of his office, of a Protestant occupational ethic of the statesman. It was correctly said by Otto Vossler that in Bismarck's sense only the "pious" man could conduct good, or practical, politics; that is, politics based on the demands of reality, not on arbitrariness. "I am," Bismarck once declared in the Chamber of Deputies, "a statesman . . . disciplined by and subject to the entire needs and demands of the state."

Thus, the personal motives and tensions in Bismarck's world of ideas and the inner form of his political thought merges with a consciousness of *service*, taking the word in its most comprehensive sense. The feeling of "standing in the breach" and of being "used up according to plan" always balanced the sovereignty of a powerful personality. This was confirmed in the tragedy that darkened the last days of the old chancellor after he had been dismissed and robbed of his "vocation." Almost nothing shook him more than the felling of the old trees in the garden of the Imperial Chancellory, with which the new course began. He himself withdrew into the darkness of the forest, which was for him a symbol of the sequence of generations and the "permanent identity."

It is evident from all this that Bismarck's realism was not empty of ideas and principles. These had their center in his relationship to the state, the role given him in the midst of the forces of history. Through his total devotion and dedication to them, they became separated to a certain degree from his person. They became part of an ethos of the state that had its historic hour. Whatever its limitations and however much the surrounding world has since changed, it is an ethos of the state to which we may not deny allegiance without shaking a basic pillar of the Western world, one that has withstood the flood of party passions since the days of the Wars of Religion.

HAJO HOLBORN (1902–   ) was a professor at
the University of Berlin and at the Berlin
Hochschule für Politik when the Nazis came to power.
He was compelled to leave Germany in 1934
because of his political convictions and became a
professor at Yale University. Holborn has written
extensively on German and European history, from
the time of the Reformation to the present. Among
his works is a three-volume *History of Modern
Germany*, which covers the whole spectrum of German
culture. His scholarship is notable for its
chronological range, the wide scope of its subject
matter, and its humanistic impulse. He began his
career with research on Bismarck and has repeatedly
returned to this subject over the years.*

► # *Champion of Monarchy*
and Aristocracy

In view of the close connection of Bismarck's work with the rise and defeat of
Germany as a world power and, even
more important, with Europe's loss of
leadership in world affairs, it is not surprising that even sixty years after his
death the figure of the German chancellor has remained shrouded in controversies. These controversies cannot be
easily settled, but we cannot hope for
progress as long as we do not clearly de-
fine the historical ideas and the political
and social movements that molded his
nature and the configuration of objective historical powers in which he acted.
Bismarck has often been described, particularly by German writers, as a man
who was not truly a member of his own

age, but rather belonged to an earlier
historic age if not to a timeless age of
heroes. Foreign students have been inclined to neglect the time-bound conditions of his growth with the result that
he has appeared more modern than he
was.

Obviously it is quite impossible to
place Bismarck outside the century on
the political fortunes of which he had a
greater impact than almost any other
person. At the same time, uniquely personal as his historical role was, Bismarck
was to some extent the beneficiary of
prior historic decisions. If it seemed in
the early part of the XIXth century that
liberalism might steadily spread from
Western to Central Europe, the success

* From Hajo Holborn, "Bismarck's Realpolitik," *Journal of the History of Ideas*, vol. 21 (1960),
pp. 84–98, omitting most of the original footnotes. Reprinted by permission of the author and
the *Journal of the History of Ideas*.

of Bismarck's policies in the 1860s brought this movement to a standstill. But the weakness of the forces of liberalism in Central Europe had already been revealed by the course of the revolutions of 1848–49, and some effective methods for subverting liberalism had been practiced by Louis Bonaparte and Prince Felix Schwarzenberg at a time when Bismarck was still in a largely meditative stage of his career.

In a famous letter to Leopold von Gerlach Bismarck expressed his belief that "nobody ever loses the stamp which the age of youthful impressions has imposed on him," and he disassociated himself from the older man who had formed his ideals during the war of liberation from Napoleon. Friedrich Meinecke already has called attention to the relatively cool attitude which Bismarck always displayed with regard to the period of Prussian reform and liberation. To be sure, the struggle against foreign domination seemed to him a worthy cause, but he denied that the simultaneous attempt of the Prussian reformers to establish an ideal German state had made an essential contribution to eventual liberation. The philosophical idealism of the age of Kant, Fichte, and Schleiermacher, in which a Stein, Humboldt, Scharnhorst, Gneisenau, and Boyen had found the expression of their own ideal longings, was alien to Bismarck.

Bismarck grew up when the German philosophy of the classic age ceased to satisfy the hearts of the young. In the years after 1815, the German philosophy had grown more scholastic, and the deep human experiences which had once led to its creation were largely hidden under a crust of abstract logical thought. The generation which began to take the stage after 1835, the year in which David Friedrich Strauss published his *Life of Jesus*, criticized idealism for its failure to understand the new reality and to give a positive direction to life. Strauss, and those after him, Ludwig Feuerbach, Bruno Bauer, and Karl Marx, all manifested the gathering trend toward realism, which with these Young-Hegelians, however, assumed at first an even more intensely rationalistic tinge than with the old Hegel.

It was this rationalism that Bismarck resented. As a youth he had received religious instruction from Schleiermacher, the warmhearted philosopher and patriotic preacher whose vindication of religion and emphasis on sentiment and feeling had meant to an earlier generation the release from the exclusive rule of reason. Bismarck discovered in Schleiermacher's teachings only an intellectualistic pantheism, which he proceeded to combine with a skepticism that denied the possibility of any human knowledge of God's plan of the world and of the place of the individual in it. This agnosticism, which according to Bismarck derived chiefly from Spinoza and the Stoics, always welled up as one important element in Bismarck's thinking, and particularly in his late years.

Bismarck's search for the concrete beauty of life never fully relieved the boredom and melancholy that his skepticism produced. He was always close to nature. His wide readings in German classic literature and most of all in Shakespeare, as well as the music of Beethoven, gave his imaginative mind models of heroic men and great tragic situations. Shakespeare had been declared the poetic genius by Herder and the young Goethe. Bismarck fully accepted the modern German outlook that originated with the literary revolution of *Sturm und Drang*. He desired passion and sentiment and, therefore, found much of the work of the romantic writers to his liking. Yet it was not the romanticism which looked for an escape from the realities into a realm of artificial beauty or of religion that attracted him, but those romantic efforts that led to a clearer grasp of reality. Through its devotion to the unique value of individuality, romanticism, indeed, prepared the ground for a more realistic study of the world, as the growth of modern historical studies in Germany showed. With sharp and piercing eyes the young Bismarck looked around in his own personal world and early revealed an extraordinary gift for literary narration and characterization.

In the school of romanticism the cult of personality flourished to excess, and in this respect also Bismarck was a true child of his age. For some time Byron was dearer to him than Shakespeare. The young Bismarck gave free reign to his pugnaciousness in dozens of duels, and he plunged headlong into stormy love affairs. Eventually he refused to enter, as a Prussian of his class was expected to do, the government services or make the army his career. "I do not like superiors," he exclaimed, and another time, "I want to make music as I like it or not at all." Thus he withdrew to the family estates, which he managed very effectively. But only part of his energies were engaged. There was time left to resume the search for the meaning of life, and even more to parade his self-confidence before the neighbors by audacious acts of sportsmanship or by extravagant pranks. The unbridled cult of individuality was threatening to corrode any serious purpose of his existence. It was his conversion to a positive theistic Christian view and his marriage, in 1847, that ended this period of life of the "mad junker," as he had been called.

Bismarck's religious conversion has been much studied. Practically no one has questioned the sincerity of his religious feelings, though many have pointed out that Bismarck's adoption of a theistic faith was closely related to his wish to be accepted by his devout future bride and her pietistic family. The sudden death of a close friend, Marie von Blankenburg, and the love for her friend Johanna von Puttkamer naturally gave his questions about life a new urgency, and the religion of his friends made a serious impression on him. Still, there was a strong voluntaristic side to Bismarck's decision. By embracing a personal God he set an end to his drifting in doubts. At the same time his marriage gave him a firm anchorage in Prussian society, in which he had his natural roots, but from which so far he had longed to flee into a world of free and heroic action. Together with his pantheism he dismissed what he occasionally called his republicanism. In the same breath he won a wife and a religious and political faith. He had chosen his fundamental position when a little later the revolution drew him into the political arena, first as a parliamentarian, subsequently as a diplomat, and finally as a minister of state.

Yet before appraising his statecraft we must stress that Bismarck did not become a Pietist in 1847. He placed his trust in a personal God, whom he accepted as the creator and king of the universe, but he obviously cared little for Christian dogmas. He prayed to God, whose ways he considered unfathomable and whom he did not think to move by his prayer. But he said—probably unaware that the words could be found in Schleiermacher's *Glaubenslehre*—that the usefulness of prayer lay in submission to a strong power. His new belief in a personal God was actually still compatible with much of Bismarck's original skepticism. Though less general, it was almost as subjective as his earlier notions. As a matter of fact, in his later years he seems to have moved even closer to his early ideas.

It was probably impossible in XIXth-century German Protestantism to find any conception of the Christian Church as a divinely ordained community which possessed a moral authority independent of the state. The Protestant Churches were essentially state-controlled institutes for preaching. The Pietists were critics of this state-system and often opposed to ministers. But all they could do was to form small conventicles such as those in which Bismarck had come in contact with Pietistic orthodoxy. Bismarck never cultivated any group worship after his conversion and favored the state-church, though he himself, as he put it, did not wish to be "edified by mouth of ministers." Yet since he suspected ministers of being desirous of power, he preferred having them under the supervision of the state. Another observation can be made. The new faith helped to give Bismarck's whole thinking a firm orientation. It also made him act not only with greater determination but also with a heightened sense of moral responsibility. Yet it did not change his relations with his fellow-men. He remained the cavalier, normally polite to his equals, well-mannered and benevolent even to members of the lesser classes, but on the other hand reckless in forcing people to serve him or humiliating them if they refused, or were suspected of refusing, co-operation. The man who lay awake whole nights "hating," who could perhaps forget but not forgive—all this according to his own

testimony—had not through his conversion become a new man.

Friedrich Meinecke has suggested that the decline of German idealism in the 1830s might be responsible for Bismarck's turning away from idealism to orthodoxy and thereby from liberalism to conservatism. He thought that if Bismarck had found a philosophy which would have answered the burning questions of his personal growth, he might have become a more liberal statesman like Cavour. Although I agree with Meinecke that the formation of Bismarck's personal convictions cannot be explained outside of his age, the question raised by Meinecke defies a solution because it is impossible to visualize different historical circumstances while assuming that the person involved would remain the same. Bismarck actually absorbed certain influences of German idealism, and the subjective and voluntaristic religion which he adopted was clearly "post-idealistic," but the liberal and humanitarian elements of the classic German philosophy found no response in him.

In 1838 the young Gladstone wrote his first book in which he pleaded for the closest relation between Church and state. Without a sanctifying principle, he argued, the state would become a mere machine with no other function than that of registering and executing opinions of the popular will like the hands of a clock. Gladstone was then still an ardent Tory, and his theses were warmly applauded by Frederick William IV of Prussia and his conservative friends. It is well known how greatly Gladstone's political views changed in his later years, when he became a liberal out of Christian convictions. But as little as he gave up his Christian belief did he deviate from his early demand that creative politics called for "sanctifying principles." Bismarck saw in Gladstone more than in any other statesman on the contemporary European scene his ideological opposite. He was wrong, however, in asserting that Gladstone—or, as he labelled him with one of his strongest vituperative expressions, *"Professor"* Gladstone—was ruining England, nor could he know that a Gladstonean Professor Wilson was destined to become the foremost destroyer of the German monarchy.

What made Bismarck a fiery enemy of Gladstone was both the liberalism and insistence of Gladstone on a Christian program in politics. Bismarck soon parted company with his early conservative associates, the members of the so-called Christian-Germanic circle, with regard to the application of Christian principles to practical politics. In Bismarck's view, the world and its orders were created by God and the course of history directed by him. The existing political institutions, consequently, were not made by men nor could they be altered by ideal constructions of human reason, as the liberals proposed. But the concrete plan of God was unknown to man, except that it was clear that in all history the decisions had been reached by power used for selfish interests, and that this *raison d'état* could be studied and acted upon. This nature of the political life of the world was to him divinely instituted and, therefore, essentially immutable, although life was a continuous conflict and struggle. To hope that men could change the nature of politics would be sinfully arrogant and would mean to meddle in divine government. The statesman might gain, however, at rare moments a fleeting

adumbration of divine action on a higher plane.

These ideas excluded the possibility of Christianizing the state and the international life. There was no ideal state, let alone an ideal international order, but only the concrete order of history which demanded from everybody obedience to the positive law. This Bismarckian attitude has been called Lutheran by historical students of Bismarck, and it is quite true that his political conceptions showed the earmarks of the political thinking that had developed in German Lutheranism. But it would be erroneous to assume that Bismarck's and Luther's opinions were identical. The world of states was for Luther not the arena for the realization of the kingdom of God. Luther admitted that statecraft required special political knowledge though to him this was not identical with the *raison d'état*. And while Luther did not believe that the state as such was a Christian institution, he considered it the duty of every individual Christian to assert within the public life a special moral attitude derived from his Christian faith. In this respect Bismarck's early conservative companions, particularly Friedrich Julius Stahl, were closer to Luther than Bismarck.

But Bismarck did not deny that at least the statesman himself, if he was a Christian, was bound by certain specific principles. The exercise of power was not to aim at personal ends but was a calling to preserve the natural order of things and to serve the state. No doubt, these were important moral restraints which reflected genuine ideas of Luther, though in somewhat weaker fashion. Luther justified war only in self-defense and recommended that Christian princes should rather suffer some occasional injustice and forget about their own "rep-utation" than go to a war that would bring calamitous suffering to their people. Bismarck repeatedly condemned preventive wars and never accepted war lightheartedly, but he did accept it as a means for accomplishing his political aims. Also, he ruled out wars for prestige, but not for the honor of the state.

The outlook on life and history with which Bismarck entered politics endowed the prevailing political conditions of Prussia with an aura of sanctity. Not only the monarchy but also the traditional class society of Prussia, with the junker estate as the dominant social group, was in his eyes the God-willed order of things, and its maintenance by all means of political cunning the unquestionable duty of the statesman. Liberalism, which for him comprised every movement derived from the ideas of the American and French Revolutions, was the sworn enemy of a healthy political life, since it attempted to replace historically developed forms of life by an arbitrary system of man-made institutions. In Bismarck's thought any kind of liberalism was bound to lead to government by parties, and this weakening of the authority of the state would bring forth the chaos of a social republic, from which a people could be freed only by a regime of fire and sword. On the other hand, a regime of naked force was disliked by Bismarck, although many governmental measures which he recommended or adopted were of highly doubtful legality. He was not even a champion of an unrestricted absolute monarchy. He objected to the suppression of the independent rights of the nobility by rulers. Moreover, absolutism fed that "boa constrictor," bureaucracy, which was tyrannical but at the same time a breeding ground of liberal notions.

These Bismarckian conceptions might have made this junker a radical reactionary after the breakdown of the German revolution, radical to the extent of demanding the suppression of those moderate German-national and liberal trends that had existed in Prussia before 1848, and even more of the concessions made during the revolution, of which the Prussian constitution of 1850 was the most important grant. But in spite of his brazenly contemptuous attitude toward democracy and liberalism during the revolution, Bismarck was not found among the extreme die-hards in the 1850s. A parliament, in particular, seemed to offer many potential advantages. Through it the conservatives could assert their views—if need be even against crown and bureaucracy—and Bismarck never forgot that the king had faltered in the early months of the revolution. But the chief value of a parliament was the chance it provided for entering on a contest with the liberal forces. Bismarck realized that these forces could not be conquered by mere repression and that the ideological errors and the political futility of modern democracy would have to be shown up by word and deed.

While Bismarck, therefore, accepted a parliament, he remained a deadly foe of parliamentary government. The monarchical government was always to retain a basis of power of its own and for this reason never surrender its exclusive control of the army and foreign affairs. During the revolution of 1848–1849 Bismarck had seen that the Austrian and Prussian monarchies recovered their strength because their armies remained loyal to the dynastic cause. He had also observed the weaknesses in German liberalism, how the fear of social revolution had impaired its aggressive spirit, how the political moderates and radicals had divided, and how the ideas about the forms of the desired national union, *grossdeutsch* vs. *kleindeutsch*, had produced further splits in German liberalism. He had also noticed that the social and economic program of the liberals failed to keep its early large following united, and that individual groups could be bought rather cheaply by the old governments. It had not escaped his attention that the majority of the German people, especially the peasant and working classes, were still politically quiescent and that it might be feasible to mobilize them for the support of monarchical government, as Louis Bonaparte had done.

These were Bismarck's formative experiences as he rose to become the leading statesman of the Prussian state. His supreme goal was and remained the preservation and the elevation of the Prussian military monarchy. He was convinced that the power of Prussia in Germany and Europe could be enhanced once her policies were freed from the shackles which the Christian principles of the old conservatism imposed. This applied not only to foreign affairs but also to domestic politics. As long as the sanction of force remained firmly in the hands of a sovereign king, he saw no danger in adopting some of the aims of what he called "the revolution." Jacob Burckhardt proved his gift of divination when, in 1872, he wrote in a letter to a friend: "Bismarck took only into his own hands what would have happened eventually, albeit without him and against him. He saw that the growing democratic-social tide would somehow produce a state of absolute violence. . . . Said he: 'I shall do it myself,' and conducted the three wars of 1864, 1866, and 1870."

"Only the kings make revolution in Prussia," Bismarck once said to Napoleon III, and on this premise he was willing to play with the devil. He felt strong enough to see to it that "God will remain master in the house and the devil can only show himself in the entrance hall, even though he may sometimes pretend there to be the lord." These words of Bismarck revealed the springs of his political actions. He freely co-operated in the diplomatic field not only with governments of revolutionary origins, if this seemed advantageous to him, but equally with revolutionary forces at home. The principle of legitimate monarchy was boldly violated by him when he dispossessed the dynasties of Hanover, Hesse-Kassel, and Nassau, in 1866, and introduced Bonapartist devices such as universal suffrage into German politics. The most crucial issue was the problem of nationalism. Bismarck's Prussian patriotism originally far outweighed his German-national sentiments. Nationalism to him smelled too much of the democratic *volonté générale* and he saw the political world grounded on historic states. But German unification offered the greatest single opportunity for the growth of Prussian power; it could not be achieved without some co-operation with the popular national movement, which might imperil the monarchical structure of the Prussian state. Only insofar as national unification could be accomplished without subordinating the Prussian crown to the rule of parties did it become a practical policy. On the other hand, if the royal government succeeded in fulfilling the national dream which the German liberals had failed to realize in 1848–1849, the national principle would strengthen conservatism, and liberalism would lose its appeal.

The political order that Bismarck created in Germany fully confirmed these fundamental thoughts and convictions. The new German Empire was built on the balance of a union of the German princes and states, represented in the chief federal organ, the *Bundesrat* or Federal Council on the one side, and the popular national movement represented in the *Reichstag* on the other. The Prussian government was still in undisputed control of the royal army and of the conduct of foreign policy; besides, it was capable of manipulating the balance between the German princes and the parties. In the decade after 1866 Bismarck leaned heavily on the largest political party, the liberal party, because he was apprehensive of the attitude of the non-Prussian particularist forces and equally of the fierce opposition of his former friends, the Prussian conservatives, to which he was exposed in this period. In order to gain the support of the liberals Bismarck made very important concessions not only in economic policy but also in the establishment of fundamental political institutions. But in the management of military and foreign affairs he brooked no interference with the absolute prerogatives of the crown. When he gained the impression that liberals might eventually gather sufficient strength to impose parliamentary government, he broke up the liberal party by buying the continued backing of the right wing with the gift of industrial protection and maneuvering the remaining left liberals into a forlorn opposition.

After 1878 the balance between the particularist and the nationalist forces was shifted. The states as represented in the Federal Council as well as the Prussian government were used as a shield to stop the further development of the central parliament. The coalition with the Prussian conservatives was thus restored and was cemented by the grant of protective import duties on agrarian products. After 1878 Bismarck also began to relax in the war which he had conducted against the Central Party in the years after 1872. Since the political movements of German Catholicism was linked up with the particularist forces and could rely on an autonomous and universal authority, the Roman Catholic Church, he had fought both the political aspirations of the German Catholics and the claims of the Roman Church. A compromise over state-church relations was developed in the course of the 1880s, and though the German government and the Center Party continued to look at each other with deep distrust, they co-operated in a good many political actions.

After national unification had been achieved, Bismarck was quick to brand everybody who opposed or criticized the new constitutional order an unpatriotic citizen, or as he expressed it, a *Reichsfeind*. While the leaders of the Center remained at least under the suspicion of being "enemies of the Empire" and the left liberals remained marked men, Bismarck saw the chief danger for the Empire after 1878 in the growing working class movement. To be sure, he met it not only by repressive measures against the Social Democratic Party but also by legislation that aimed at the alleviation of the conditions of the industrial worker. But when these positive social policies, which were conceived in a paternalistic spirit, failed to produce immediate results, he prepared for a showdown with the Social Democrats in 1890. In the expectation that the *Reichstag* might make the suppression of the Social Democratic Party impossible, Bismarck began to consider concrete plans for a *coup d'état* which was intended to create a docile federal parliament. German constitutionalism was certainly on unsafe grounds, and Max Weber's description of the Bismarckian-system as "pseudo-constitutionalism" seems historically correct.

Bismarck's fall in 1890 was connected with these issues, though it was essentially caused by the desire of William II to rule by himself. By one simple stroke the young emperor was able to remove not only the founder of the Empire but also with him the leading rôle of the ministers, which Bismarck had considered necessary for the formulation of prudent policies in a modern monarchy. But he had overrated his personal capacity for keeping the trust of the monarch and never contemplated the problem of his succession earnestly enough. In the years after his dismissal Bismarck began to clamor for the strengthening of the parliament which, while in power, he had done his best to make impotent. Another major weakness of his policies became apparent only in the era of William II. As mentioned before, Bismarck deeply resented the power of bureaucracy in government. He saw in bureaucracy a force that tended to disregard traditional class lines and regional differences in the light of a concept of law applicable to every citizen of the state. Actually, Bismarck's semi-absolutistic state could not have existed without a bureaucracy, and the extension of governmental functions to many new fields in the absence of a marked increase of self-government was bound to proliferate bureaucratic rule. Bismarck's critical attitude toward bureaucracy resulted merely in the weeding out of men of liberal character, and the personal regime of William II inherited a civil service of unusually servile and spineless behavior. Bismarck himself knew quite clearly the foundation of power on which he had placed the Prussian kings. At the last meeting with William II in 1897 the old man remarked, pointing to the military officers of the imperial entourage, that the Emperor would be able to act as he pleased just as long as he had such an officer corps behind him. Indeed, the Empire of Bismarck and William II collapsed only when the German army was defeated.

Bismarck's statecraft was called *Realpolitik*[1] already by his contemporaries, particularly by those German liberals who after 1866 were eager to make their

[1] The term *Realpolitik* became fashionable under the influence of the book *Grundsätze der Realpolitik, angewendet auf die staatlichen Zustände Deutschlands*, published by August Ludwig Rochau in 1853. As a student Rochau had participated in the abortive Frankfurt *putsch* of 1833. A fugitive from a life sentence he lived for fifteen years in France where he came in contact with the new French sociology. The revolution of 1848 brought Rochau back to Germany. In his book Rochau argued that what gravity is in nature, power is in politics. But although Rochau was an advocate of German unification through Prussian leadership, the power which he had in mind was social rather than military power. The state could gain strength only by allying itself with the strongest forces of society, and power today rested with the bourgeoisie. Rochau wanted to achieve German unification through constitutional reform. It was logical that he became, in 1859, the secretary of the *Deutsche National-alverein*, which fought and criticized Bismarck until 1866 from a liberal point of view. . . . In spite of the enthusiastic reception given to it by the young Treitschke, Rochau's book was very quickly forgotten. But the term *Realpolitik* remained current and either denoted a policy contemptuous of all ideals and ideologies and following the interests of the state or it was merely identified with a policy exclusively employing power for the achievement of its ends. The word has become misleading on account of its ambiguities; historically it should not be used, in my opinion, except for the statesmen who entered the scene in the decade after 1848, and even then it calls for exact definition.

peace with Bismarck even if this implied the abandonment of most of their political faith. There was great comfort in having been shown wrong not by a straight-line conservative partisan but by a man above ideologies. Bismarck himself promoted such sentiments. He was quite sincere when he made many confessions like the following: "If I had to go through life with principles, I would feel as though I had to walk a narrow path in the woods and had to carry a long pole in my mouth." He never tired of emphasizing that the statesman could not impose his will on the course of history, but that on the contrary the general developments forced his hands. Realistic observation of existing political conditions and the ability to wait for the right moment of intervention were absolute prerequisites of any political action. Moreover, since the counteraction of others and the fluctuating configuration of political forces could never be predicted with certainty, it was always advisable to hold more than one policy ready in order to be prepared for shifting circumstances.

Bismarck possessed the ability of keeping two or more irons in the fire as well as an acute sense of timing, and he was masterly in recognizing and analyzing the power factors of any given situation. He was profoundly conscious of the fact that the political craft was "the art of the possible." This goes far to explain his great success as a statesman, but it does not explain the character of his policies. Bismarck was not a mere opportunist who simply responded to events as they unfolded. It is quite wrong to assume that he had a fully developed plan of German unification, roughly identical with his subsequent policies, when he became Prussian prime minister in 1862. Actually he considered various

solutions as late as 1866, and he hesitated for a long time to play for the high stakes which were involved in the war with Austria. But all his policies, the ones contemplated and the ones enacted, had their general unity and ultimate purpose in firm principles which were to him unchangeable ideals. While he denied any human capacity to improve the nature of politics by the application of Christian or liberal ideas, he believed religiously in the duty of the statesman to conserve a state independent of popular forces.

Bismarck applied these principles not only to national but also to international policies. In the preservation of the Habsburg monarchy as a great power after Sadowa and the close cooperation with Russia, it was his chief objective to stem the progress of the movement of nationalities in eastern Europe. He was afraid that these national states would be of revolutionary character. The existence of the three historic empires seemed to him also a necessity for the maintenance of peace in Europe. Under parliamentary government a stable foreign policy was continuously imperilled by shifting majorities. But the three emperors still held full control over foreign and military affairs. To bring them into a lasting league was the chief endeavor of Bismarck after 1871, and perhaps already after 1866. In the chapter of his memoirs in which he epitomizes the intention of his policy of alliances, he describes his attempt to build a league of the three emperors as having been motivated by the expectation of an imminent struggle between the two European movements, named by Napoleon the Republican and the Cossack party. He goes on to say that he would rather describe them in present-day terms as "the system of order on a monarchical basis in opposition to the social republic into which the anti-monarchical movement, slowly or by leaps usually sinks."

The historian can point out that successful as Bismarck's diplomacy was up to 1890, it did not solve all the problems of the future. Monarchical succession may produce even greater freakishness than varying parliamentary majorities. As a matter of fact, diplomatic relations between Germany and Russia grew more difficult under Alexander III than they had been under Alexander II, and the rising pan-slavism gained in influence on the decisions of the czarist regime in foreign affairs. In Austria-Hungary the imperial government proved powerless to check the continuous growth of national movements. Bismarck, although not unaware of the developments in Russia and Austria-Hungary, tended rather to minimize their significance. He persuaded himself too easily that the Austrian monarchy still had the power to curb, through a *coup d'état*, the nationalities by abrogating the constitutional rights which it had conceded after 1861. These were signs that his diplomatic aims rested not only on the realistic appraisal of events but also on strong political convictions.

In contrast to classical liberalism Bismarck did not conceive of the state as the representative of the nation. Nor did he follow Hegel, who accepted absolutist governments but saw in the state the embodiment of a national culture. This view presupposed at the very least some causal interaction between the progress of a national civilization and the life of the state. Bismarck's concept of the state excluded all forces which might interfere with the independent authority vested in the king. The state was for him identical with the monarch and those men needed to maintain and

exercise his sovereignty, primarily the noblemen serving in the king's army and councils. Such an authoritarian political philosophy could gain popular support as long as the churches preached obedience to the established social and political order and the people readily accepted Christian teachings. But the Roman Catholic social theory, though anti-revolutionary, was far from anti-critical, and *vis-à-vis* the Prussian monarchy the German Catholics had good reasons to keep a reserved attitude even before the *Kulturkampf*. The Protestant Churches, on the other hand, had lost their hold on the German urban population.

Bismarck's theory of state and government was ill-suited to serve as the political creed of the non-Prussian groups included in the new Empire, and even less of the new classes which the modern industrial expansion created. Bismarck himself was incapable of understanding the yearnings for a higher human dignity which expressed themselves in liberalism and social democracy as well as in the political ideals of German Catholicism. To him all these political theories were subversive. He denied to the parties any participation in the government and kept them divided among themselves by fomenting antagonism over economic interests. The founder of the unified Empire failed to unify the people. Bismarck knew about this lack of integration. Conscious of the need for mass-support he turned to nationalism. In a letter written to Prince William half-a-year before the latter's accession to the imperial throne, he said "the national idea is stronger than the Christian idea, even among Social-Democrats and other democrats, maybe not in the country, but in the cities." From 1871 on Bismarck used increasingly national tones in his public utterances. He did not use the language of liberal nationalism but liked to talk of the perennial qualities of the German race which he discovered in all of German history and Teutonic pre-history. Here it was demonstrated that the Germans had always prospered when they followed their kings and exhibited their best virtues, such as supreme bravery, to support their leaders. There was also the reverse side, the stories about the endemic party spirit that ever so often had spelled disaster to the nation. Bismarck was far removed from the biological materialism of the National-Socialist racial theory. He drew distinctions between "masculine" and "feminine" races and asserted that the best people were those produced from a mixture of the two. Happily, the Prussians, with their strong Slav admixture, fitted into such a pattern. Also Bismarck's anti-semitism was rather undogmatic and derived largely from class-consciousness and Christian antipathy. Yet he was already affected by the new naturalism or social Darwinism when he described the world of political power as mirroring nature, in which eternal war went on among lower and higher animals and the stronger prevailed. Ernst Troeltsch has shown how easily such naturalistic views could be grafted on the social teachings of Lutheranism. Lutheranism declared it to be the divine will that governmental authority in this world had to rest on power and since the individual had no recourse from the abuse of power to ethical principles, it was tempting to describe secular history in naturalistic terms.

Thus the lack of political ideas on which the loyalties of the large masses of the modern age might have been built aided the promotion of political ideologies which did not represent the full scope of Bismarck's thinking. A new German generation was quick to fasten upon the nationalist ideas of Bismarck and expand on them. At the same time a legendary Bismarck grew up and was immortalized in the innumerable statues of him, erected between 1890 and 1914 on German city squares and hill-sites. In these monuments Bismarck appears as the fearless military Empire-builder and stony Teutonic hero, but they reveal nothing of the spiritual German heritage which helped to form his personality.

HERMANN ONCKEN (1869–1946) wrote two notable
biographies (on Rudolf von Bennigsen and
Ferdinand Lassalle) and was the editor and author
of a number of works on German diplomatic history.
He began his research on the "Rhine policy" of
Napoleon III soon after the Versailles Treaty had
deprived Germany of Alsace-Lorraine and the Saar—
and at a time also when French occupation of the
Rhineland had excited new fears in Germany of
France's ambition to detach the region from Germany.
Some historians have charged that the three volumes
of documents which he collected and published
on the subject do not fully support the thesis he
advances in the introduction to this work, from
which the following selection is taken.*

► ## Napoleon: France's Drive Toward the Rhine

With soldierly frankness the French military attaché in Berlin, Colonel Stoffel, discussed the true cause of the war at the time of its outbreak. He said that the war was the result of the preponderance of Prussia since 1866 and that this preponderance required France to secure her boundaries. Such security, he felt, she could attain only by acquiring the German territory west of the Rhine, and French possession of the Rhine alone could guarantee the peace between the two nations. These utterances are in agreement with the facts as we have revealed them according to the documents, except that the documents go even farther and show that already prior to the war of 1866 Napoleon had a Rhine policy and by an unsuccessful intrigue had himself helped to establish the order which later he believed he could subvert only by conquering the Rhine. This is corroborated by the fact that as late as August 6, the day of the battle of Wörth, Prince Metternich, who had a deeper insight than anyone else into the Napoleonic policies of 1863–1870, spoke outright of the Rhine as the chief war aim. This fact, usually kept dark in France nowadays, was emphasized on September 18, 1919, by the French socialist J. Longuet in a parliamentary address, when he said that it should not be forgotten that the yearning for the left bank of the Rhine was responsible for the war of 1870.

* From *Napoleon III and the Rhine*, by Hermann Oncken, pp. 183–194. Copyright 1928 by Alfred A. Knopf, Inc. Reprinted by permission.

In July, 1870, to be sure, French diplomacy had to speak a quite different language abroad. The louder the rabble in Paris clamored for the Rhine, the more zealously did France try to make the outside world believe that she was waging no war of aggression. Although there was little enough serious hope of winning over the South German states, the French government, in all declarations made prior to the final decision of South Germany, made a particular point of stating that it did not intend to take an inch of German soil and wished merely to check the further growth of Prussia. Gramont[1] even went so far as expressly to disavow to the Bavarian minister the demands for the Rhine voiced by the Paris press and was careful to have this noble renunciation loudly proclaimed especially in the Viennese press; so that public sentiment in German Austria might not be estranged but might be prepared for a war on the side of France.

But did these formal declarations, which culminated in Napoleon's war manifesto of July 23, contain the whole truth, or did they admit of evasion and doubtful interpretation? It has already been mentioned that Denmark was to receive as the minimum price of her cooperation all of Schleswig—in other words territory of distinctly German stamp which had been hotly contested for a generation. And what the French were prepared to offer Austria in the event of cooperation, is clear from the negotiations carried on ever since 1866. There can be no doubt that in case of victory not only Silesia would have changed hands; it is more than likely that the old Austrian craving for Bavarian territory would have cropped up

[1] The Duke of Gramont, French Foreign Minister after May 15, 1870.—*Ed.*

again too. And what of the specifically French war objectives?

While publicly stressing non-annexation, Paris found it necessary to resort once more to the substitute for pure annexation which it had for years advocated as a solution compatible with German self-respect and national consciousness, and sugared with so many secret hopes. The autonomous Rhineland state appears once more as a French war aim in the decisive hour. At any rate the French minister in Stuttgart allowed this rather obscure remark to escape him: according to the plans made in Paris in the last few years it is the French aim, in case of victory, to establish a state of about five million inhabitants along the Rhine, perhaps for the King of Hannover." Gramont too spoke to the Bavarian minister of a restoration and enlargement of Hannover in order to destroy the Prussian preponderance. Although he considered it more expedient not to mention the Rhineland state expressly, he revealed his intention in another way by hinting at the "annulment" of Baden as a Prussian subsidiary. It will be remembered that it was Gramont too who as early as April, 1867, had offered the Austrians South Germany as far as the Black Forest and had shown a special French interest only for Baden. These few points will suffice to disclose the extent of French "renunciation" with respect to German soil. In reverting to the old idea of a neutral state along the Rhine, as a policy which ought to prove acceptable to Europe, France realized of course that in case the treaty of peace were really dictated in Berlin, this modest policy, which was always considered a minimum requirement, would not have to stand.

But the French revealed not only individual phases of their war program. At one point they developed the program in its entirety, though in a discreet form. We refer to the declaration which Gramont early in August was indiscreet enough to make to the Russian chargé in official form, describing it expressly as containing the minimum demands of France. This list includes annexation pure and simple. In demanding the cession of the Saar basin Gramont clearly violated the solemn promise not to claim even a bit of German territory. As for the boundaries of 1814, which ever since 1860 were regarded as the most modest satisfaction of French needs, French diplomacy was accustomed to regard them as resting on an old legal title. But the sum total of the German territorial modifications, which France communicated without hesitation to this friend of Prussia, is even more impressive. It included the reduction of Prussia to the boundaries of 1866 and restoration of the dispossessed; enlargement of the middle states at the expense of ancient Prussian territory, and "constitution of state groups in Germany which would permanently break the Prussian supremacy." This formula expresses the well-known aim of dividing Germany into as many equally large states as possible, the aim which had been made the basis of the Franco-Austrian negotiations of 1869. No evidence is necessary to prove that in this grouping the neutralized Rhineland state with a generous allotment of territory was to play an important part and would in a sense have symbolized the federalistic dismemberment of Germany.

In one respect the war aims communicated by Gramont to the Russians contain a surprise—a feature which at the same time explains the reason why they were communicated at all. At the end of the French minister asked the Russian government the official question what it

planned to do if the French army should reach Berlin and offer Danzig to Russia in return for her neutrality. This free disposition of German territory, which thus revealed designs even against the eastern German frontier, is the last official expression of the French war aims, made only a short time before the first skirmish at Weissenburg.

In the light of all these French plans, which, be it noted, must be regarded as minimum demands, it becomes clear how perfidious was the war manifesto wherein Napoleon announced to the world his desire that "the peoples forming the great Germanic nation shall be free to control their own destinies." The announcement of the manifesto that it was planned to establish an order "guaranteeing our security for the future" is of the same ilk. The persistent use of such phrases for centuries did not serve to make them more plausible. The picture of the Germany of the Peace of Westphalia, exposed on every side to invasion and disruption, and with all internal bonds loosened to a degree of utter defenselessness—this was the historical ideal of the past which dominated the plans of the present. It was "the great idea" of the French policy, according to Thiers,[2] to disorganize the German state to such an extent that security and aggrandizement would fall to the happy lot of its French neighbor.

Against this menace, which had barely been avoided in 1866, the Germans had to defend their unity and independence in 1870. In this latter year it was the last echo of those Napoleonic speculations which we discovered as being the

[2] Adolphe Thiers, a spokesman for the opposition in the French parliament under Napoleon III. After the latter's defeat and the revolution which followed, he became the "chief of the executive power" of the new French government in Bordeaux.—*Ed.*

secret forces impelling the empire for the seven years between 1863 and 1870. But during a more recent period of seven years, from 1919 to 1926, we have learned by experience that the rhythm of French history is still guided by its initial principle, that this nation, impelled by the force of tradition, can not resist the evil temptations which surround it.

The policy of Napoleon and the French, which opposed Germany's national right of self-determination, led to the war of 1870. Was it justifiable for this policy to defend its fateful course of action before the bars of history by pleading the "security" of France? Is such justification admissible? We have seen how after 1866 the motive of security gradually met the requirements of the new situation and supplanted that of aggrandizement. But it was only a new name for an old concept—the concept of national frontiers, Romano-Gallic reminiscences, pseudo-historical feudal rights and other attempts to clothe gross reality in a palliating mantle of ideas. Two generations earlier the attainment of the national frontiers had been looked upon in France as a sacred tradition. "It is the doctrine of the scholar," said Sorel, "the creed of the poet, the ambition of the popular leader, of the kings the ministers the generals the political meetings and the committees; it is a question of interests for the economist, a reason of state for the politician, a national dream." All these spheres of life forthwith seized upon the motive of security, and thus revived once more a great historical tradition. This tradition, though it spoke in terms of defence, had in reality an offensive purpose, for it strove to disturb or diminish the national unity of its neighbor. It was animated by the theory that its own security, unity and peace could be maintained only if that neighbor were doomed to insecurity, disunity and unrest, and in advocating this theory it violated the unwritten law of morality which guides the life of nations and sets bounds to the egoism of national interests.

The struggles of the past are of interest for the historical consciousness of the European nations only when their motives and impulses live on in the present as a determining factor. The line which runs from Louis XIV directly to Napoleon III becomes in the end a prime cause for the war of 1870–1871. This fact was clear to the generation which fought that war. To the numerous judgments of other nations we may add the opinion of the American minister Bancroft, the renowned historian. On October 12, 1870, he spoke the following confidential words in the Berlin foreign office: "The leading statesmen as well as public opinion in America regard the present war essentially as an act of self-defence on Germany's part, and the outstanding task is to insure Germany permanently, by a better system of frontiers, against new wars of aggression on the part of her western neighbors, of which the past three centuries have brought so large a number."[3]

The real facts began to be obscured when, with the formation of the great coalition against Germany, the French conception was adopted by the political allies of France. And since the World War the question of the causes of the war of 1870 was, for political reasons, still more obscured and supplanted by a legend which described the latter as merely a step preliminary to the former. The causes of both wars were merged

[3] Undersecretary von Thile to the minister in Washington, Baron von Gerolt. Strictly confidential, October 13, 1870 (Berlin Foreign Office).

in one large question of guilt, so presented that those who, in France or in countries intellectually dependent upon her, believed in the exclusive or principal responsibility of Germany for the World War, were led to believe also the legend that France was attacked by Germany in 1870. But while the French undertook to reconstruct a fictitious past and to invent the story of the French lamb and the German wolf, it happened that the newly aroused spirit of their historical Rhineland policy, endowed with a new halo and unhampered by diplomatic considerations, has in recent years since the World War given ever more damaging testimony of them. What we have detected as the secret motive power of French politics ever since 1815 and as the Napoleonic ambition which from 1863 on led to the catastrophe, now became more irresistible than ever before. Almost all parties, with a few exceptions, now endorsed the claim for the Rhine, and all along the line scholarship, animated by a spirit which Albert Sorel had once castigated, argued the historical right of that claim, enlisting self-interest and sentiment in the service of a consistent endeavor, which varied but in the details of method and advocated now annexation pure and simple and now some form of Rhineland state, either neutral or at least independent of Prussia and in any case exposed to pene-

tration. This device, of course, had always been the first step toward conquest, and during the dark days of confusion after 1919 it found, even in Germany, sympathetic fools and treacherous advocates who did not realize whose interests would be served by any change in the established order along the Rhine.

If the causes of the war of 1870 are to be linked and associated with those of the World War, well and good. History justifies such a procedure, but not in the sense in which the enemies of Germany, who would make her alone responsible for the World War, interpret it. The French national tradition which drove Napoleon III into the war and brought about the fateful clash between the historical Rhineland policy of the French and the right of self-determination of the German people is the cradle of that spirit of revenge which played so important a part in bringing about the international tension leading to the World War. The same spirit which inspired the secret forces of the French national soul has imposed upon it a large measure of guilt before the bars of mankind. Inasmuch as this spirit prevents a permanent reconciliation of the two nations after the catastrophe, it has remained to this day the most serious obstruction to all hopes for future pacific intercourse among the nations of Europe.

Although he began his career as a lawyer,
ERICH EYCK (1878–1964) became a significant
historian of modern Germany. Compelled to leave
Germany in 1937, he settled in Great Britain, where he
lectured at Oxford and London universities. He
wrote a three-volume biography of Bismarck which
was published in Switzerland during World War II.
It was followed by other notable volumes on
Kaiser William II and the Weimar Republic. While
appreciating Bismarck's redoubtable talents, Eyck
is generally critical of his historical influence, an
interpretation that has received many adverse
reviews in Germany.*

Bismarck: A Trap Set for Napoleon

For Bismarck, it was a requirement of *raison d'état* that the Hohenzollerns establish and maintain their candidacy for the Spanish throne. *Could this end without war?* It is obvious that Bismarck calculated from the beginning on the *possibility of war*, and that in his heart he approved of this possibility. That is a state of affairs which jurists characterize as *dolus eventualis*. But here we are concerned with something more, the *intent* to unleash war. One has to speak of such an intent if Bismarck believed it *out of the range of possibility* that the Hohenzollern candidacy could have a *peaceful* outcome.

The problem reduces itself, therefore, to the question of whether Bismarck could have thought it possible that the French, without resorting to arms would permit a Hohenzollern to ascend the Spanish throne. To this one can only say that if Bismarck thought Prussian *raison d'état* demanded that a Hohenzollern be king of Spain, he must also have realized that by the same token French *raison d'état* demanded that this be hindered. Certainly the motive of Prussian *raison d'état* was to weaken France by artificially creating a threat on its Pyrenees border. Bismarck makes this clear enough in his report to the king of March 9, [1870]. To believe that the French would permit themselves to be weakened, he would have had to assume that Napoleon would follow a policy as

* Translated by Otto Pflanze from the work *Bismarck, Leben und Werk*, vol. 2, by Erich Eyck, published by Eugen Rentsch Verlag, Erlenbach n/Zürich, in 1943. Pp. 478–488. Footnotes omitted.

yielding as that of Haugwitz in 1805–1806, which historians blame for the Prussian defeat at Jena.[1] Certainly Bismarck believed in the peaceful attitude of Napoleon as well as of the great majority of the French people. But he also knew how Napoleon depended for the security of his throne on prestige in foreign policy, how badly that prestige had suffered from his repeated diplomatic defeats after 1866, and with what applause the French legislature had responded to the warning of Thiers that not another mistake could be tolerated. And what mistake could the French people have felt more strongly than the sufferance of a member of the House of Hohenzollern in Madrid, *of a diplomatic and perhaps military encirclement?* Bismarck surely saw with complete clarity what was evident to every ordinary observer; namely, that the selection of a Spanish king from the House of Hohenzollern would force Napoleon to choose between the alternatives of *war or the fall of his dynasty.* How could Bismarck have thought it conceivable that the French emperor would choose the latter?

It has been objected that if Bismarck had sought a cause for war he would certainly have sought one capable of inflaming national passions in Germany and that the Hohenzollern candidacy for Spain was clearly not suitable for that purpose. Even without being so presumptuous as to try to uncover Bismarck's secret thoughts, we can safely assume that he expected Napoleon to turn against Spain and fall into conflict with it. . . . Is it not possible that Bismarck was confident that he could find ways and means of stirring German national sentiment if it was a question of coming to the help of the Spaniards in a war begun by the French because they did not want to let a German prince rule in Spain?

The following consideration is still more important: *where at that time was a German-national cause for war against France to be found?* German unity was not yet established: the Main line was not yet crossed. But was this the fault of France? The decisive reason was that the majority of the south Germans rejected unity under Prussian leadership. Baden was the only exception. For Baden's sake alone, however, Bismarck did not want to go to war against France, and for good reason. In such a war Bavaria and Württemberg would presumably not have fought against France. Roggenbach,[2] who often went his own way and who, in contrast to the majority of Baden liberals, rejected the idea of Baden's entering the North German Confederation at that time, wrote a letter to Treitschke in February 1870 in which he doubted that Prussia would have the support of Germany if it wished to make an attempt on its own to unite Germany, and thereby brought about a conflict with Europe. But Bismarck forbade such a "spontaneous attempt at unity" for yet another reason. Any attack on Württemberg would have made the *tsar* an opponent of Prussia, and this would have affected *Bismarck's European policy* at its most critical point.

On the other hand, the French government handled the German question with great restraint. Daru was still minister of foreign affairs at the time that Bismarck first began forcefully to advocate the Hohenzollern candidacy to the

---

[1] Battle of October 14, 1806, in which Prussia was decisively defeated by Napoleon I. During the preceding year Count Christian von Haugwitz, Prussian foreign minister, had permitted his country to be isolated by Napoleon.—*Ed.*

[2] Franz von Roggenbach, foreign minister of the principality of Baden (1861–1865).—*Ed.*

king of Prussia in his memorandum of March 9, [1870]. A few days before, Daru had answered an interpellation of Jules Favres[3] with an outspoken avowal of peace, and even Werther[4] repeatedly reported how Daru had exerted himself to prevent any discussion in the Chamber of Deputies that could be interpreted as intervention in German affairs. Ollivier[5] himself went so far as to permit the publication, in the *Kölnische Zeitung* on March 13, of an interview with the German journalist Dr. Levysohn, in which he said that France would not intervene if German unity should some day come from a great popular movement *rather than from one artificially arrangéd*. It will have to be affirmed, therefore, that Bismarck initiated his Spanish policy, with all of its dangers of war, at a time when a German national outcry for war against France did not exist. Therefore this argument raised against Bismarck's desire for war collapses.

Bismarck, particularly in his old age, repeatedly characterized the war against France as necessary for the completion of German unity. In his famous speech of July 30, 1892 to the delegation of the University of Jena, he justified this view as follows: *"Without defeating France, we could never have created a German Reich* in the center of Europe and have raised it to the power it possesses today. Perhaps France would have found allies *later* with whom to prevent us from doing this; therefore, the French war was a necessary outcome."* In private conversation Bismarck, citing Cavour as an ex-

ample, claimed for the German nation the right to unleash a European war in order to attain national unity. To be sure, his purpose on these occasions was only to justify his conduct after Leopold's renunciation of the throne;[6] yet his arguments have wider implications. They were completely suited for justifying Bismarck in his own eyes if he had indeed advanced the Spanish question *from the beginning* as a "trap for Napoleon."

But was there really no other way to achieve German unity? Must one accept the depressing thought that it was only attainable by way of bloody battlefields? If the German people had really wanted it, if the whole of southern Germany had earnestly striven for entry into a united German Reich, France would not have been able to stop them. It is true that France did hold firmly to the Main line, but the will to go to war in order to maintain it grew steadily weaker. That will, moreover, would necessarily have declined further as the system of Ollivier established itself and as Napoleon's health began to fail. Napoleon never wanted to conduct a war without allies, least of all a war against a united Germany, of whose dangers he was well aware. Furthermore, the secret negotiations [with Austria] during 1869 had shown him clearly that there was no ally to be had for an aggressive war against

---

[3] Jules Favre, a leader of the liberal opposition in the French parliament.—*Ed.*

[4] Karl von Werther, ambassador of the North German Confederation in Paris.—*Ed.*

[5] Émile Ollivier, appointed French premier in late December 1869 when the Third Empire was converted into a parliamentary monarchy. —*Ed.*

[6] Leopold von Hohenzollern-Sigmaringen, of the south German branch of the Hohenzollern family, was the choice of the Spanish government for the vacant Spanish throne. On July 12, 1870, his father, Charles Anthony, withdrew his son's candidacy when premature publicity provoked a sharp reaction in Paris. Bismarck was angered by this decision, which was made without his knowledge, and by the prospect it raised of a diplomatic defeat at the hands of France. Historians are agreed that, whatever Bismarck's previous intent, he now preferred to go to war rather than accept such a defeat.—*Ed.*

Germany. The energy with which Beust[7] had insisted on Austria's right to neutrality in such a case must have robbed him of every illusion about this. An Italian alliance, on the other hand, would require the cession of Rome, a price which Napoleon felt himself unable to pay for reasons of domestic politics. In his Jena speech Bismarck spoke only of the possibility that France could have found allies in *later* years; hence he was convinced that in 1870 she did *not yet* have them. Obviously he did not accept as his own the justification given by some historians that he acted in order to forestall a threatening offensive from the other side.

Hence one can say, with as much certainty as is generally attainable in such questions, that France would not have hindered a unification of the German people *if the German people as a whole had themselves wanted it.* But precisely this prerequisite was lacking. Therefore we must ascertain the reasons why it was lacking and whether popular support for unification could not have been obtained in any way other than through a victorious war with a foreign foe.

The decisive reason was certainly not the disinclination of large segments of the southern German population for German unification as such. Concern for the preservation of Bavarian or Württemberg sovereignty played a large role only at the courts. Among the people themselves the *aversion to the Prussian military state* had an incomparably stronger influence. They looked upon the North German Confederation as but an extension of this Prussian military state, which seemed to be symbolized by

the general's uniform worn by the Confederate chancellor even at the sessions of the Reichstag. It was feared that entry into this union would mean militarization and Prussianization. Thousands of liberal-minded southern Germans would have had nothing against becoming subjects of a larger commonwealth, but they were opposed to becoming subjects of *the Prussian crown*. The latter was in their eyes the embodiment of a military dictatorship, which was more concealed than limited by parliamentary forms and which found its real support in an aristocratic officer caste that seemed completely alien to themselves. They had not yet forgotten that the Prussian government had forced its own will upon the people contrary to the constitution, that it had conducted a German civil war opposed by public opinion.

This view of the Prussian monarchy was strengthened by the character of the North German constitution, in which the attempt was made to place the power of decision in military questions completely outside the reach of parliament. The army's "iron budget" appeared to be typical of the Prussian monarchy. . . .

It was precisely this [authoritarian] position of the Prussian monarchy that Bismarck wished above all to maintain. It was not that he overvalued the political capacity of the king. On the contrary, it would hardly be possible to speak about the king more deprecatingly and contemptuously than Bismarck did. His complaint about the "notable limitation and stubbornness" of the king is by no means his most severe criticism. Nor does his characterization of the crown prince as the "most stupid and vain of men" testify to an exaggerated monarchical feeling. Yet he saw in the unlimited military power of the king the *key to domination of the entire state* and *under no circumstances* did he want to let *parliament* infringe this power. Robert Morier, a foreign observer who was as perceptive as he was critical, and who was especially well-informed, called the army Bismarck's *talisman*, which had to be kept in the hands of the executive, that is, the king. A short conversation between Bismarck and General Schweinitz in May 1870 shows how basic Bismarck's feelings were in this matter. Schweinitz, at that time Prussian minister in Vienna, remarked, "Our power reaches its limit where we run out of Junkers to occupy the officer posts in the army." To this Bismarck replied, *"I ought not to say it, but I have acted on that principle."* One can imagine the consequences if this statement had become publicly known at the time. Would it not have been answered by the cry of a thousand voices from southern Germany, "That is the Germany we do *not* want."

Yet even in northern Germany, which was now undisputedly in the Prussian sphere of influence, a struggle was in prospect concerning the army. Elections for the Reichstag were approaching. In view of the mood of the country it was not likely that the new Reichstag, which would have to deliberate over the first military budget since 1867, would be ready to say yes and amen to all demands. Even among the National Liberals there was a strong group that wished to protect the rights of the Reichstag. . . .

The war with France rescued Bismarck from all of these problems. The new Reichstag, elected in March 1871 under the influence of the magnificent victories, granted an undiminished military budget, effective not just for one but for three years. The anti-Prussian south Germans were a dwindling minority. Still it would be idle to assert that Bismarck brought about the war with France in order to overcome these obstacles. In a letter of February 1874, in which he analyzes Bismarck's difficulties in early 1870, Morier declared that it would be the task of future historians to determine through research whether these problems had any causal connection with Bucher's secret mission to Spain. Even today, seventy years after the events, the historian has to admit that this cannot be determined. Not a single word from Bismarck, no matter how confidential, gives us a clue to the answer. On the contrary, one has to remember his declaration in the crown council of 1866 against the idea that the solution to domestic political difficulties should be sought in war.

But that does not alter the fact that if there was a peaceful way for the completion of German unification, Bismarck *did not want to take* it for reasons of *domestic* politics. Both Bismarck and his times had changed greatly since his speech against the Paulskirche in April 1849 in which he declared, "I do *not* want German unity with this constitution." Yet he remained constant in this: he did not want German unity if it meant *reduction of the power of the Prussian crown.* This danger would be eliminated, for a generation at least, if German unity was the result of a war in which the Hohenzollern monarchy led the German people to victory.

All these considerations lead to the conclusion that Lothar Bucher was absolutely correct when he described the candidacy for the Spanish throne as a trap Bismarck had set for Napoleon in order to put him in an embarrassing situation from which there was no escape other than a declaration of war. . . .

Of all the wars of the nineteenth century none had nearly such lasting and far-reaching consequences as the German-French war of ˙1870–1871. Seven decades have gone by, but its effect remains. It sowed a harvest of hate and discord which far exceeded the most dour expectations of the blackest pessimists. It sealed the fate of uncounted men who were born long after the sound of the last shot had echoed away. In a moment of depression Bismarck once accused himself, "Without me three great wars would never have occurred; eighty thousand men would not have died; and parents, brothers, sisters, and widows would not have mourned." Yet how low few are these eighty thousand compared with those sacrificed indirectly as a result of this war. Two world wars have come from it, and no one can say when Europe or the world will regain the peace that ended on July 13, 1870.

This selection is from an important doctoral dissertation written by JOCHEN DITTRICH (1917–   ) under the supervision of Gerhard Ritter at the University of Freiburg. Dittrich had access to the Hohenzollern family archives in Sigmaringen, and he was also able to make use of the documents discovered after World War II in the captured archives of the German Foreign Office. Dittrich is obviously eager to rise above nationalistic bias and to treat the problem objectively. He sees the war as the result of a conflict of interests rather than of warlike intent on the part of either Bismarck or the French.*

► Conflicting Diplomatic Offensives

There is still another interpretation to consider, that of Erich Eyck. According to Eyck, Bismarck sought to confront the French emperor with the alternatives of war or the fall of the Napoleonic dynasty. Since Bismarck could not have believed that Napoleon would be reconciled to his own downfall, he must have steered with complete awareness into a war that was allegedly necessary because he had no other way to coerce the German states into accepting Prussian leadership.

French as well as German historians, absorbed in seeking the answers to subtle questions of detail and in a transparent effort to burden the other side with guilt, have almost always forgotten to point out the tragedy behind the struggle for supremacy in Europe. Perhaps it could be asked, "Why could not the French simply permit the unification of Germany?" They would say, "We feared for our security and justifiably so, as two world wars have shown." We could reply that this grave development was first begun by French resistance to German unification. The conflict of 1870–1871 raised the problem of Alsace-Lorraine and led to the growth of hatred that indirectly helped to unleash the last two wars. Yet the question is rather unrealistic. What state has ever willingly relinquished its own position of power as long as it saw a chance to defend it? On the other hand, what people will let

* From Jochen Dittrich, *Bismarck, Frankreich und die Spanische Thronkandidatur der Hohenzollern* (Munich: R. Oldenbourg Verlag, 1962), pp. 43, 71–82, omitting the original footnotes. Translated by Otto Pflanze. By permission of R. Oldenbourg Verlag.

itself be deprived of the right to determine its own way of life without a struggle? It is in the nature of the power struggle between states that some issues transcend their immediate context and become matters of fate. This may be regrettable, but who has yet been able to make it otherwise? . . .

Bismarck's policy toward France during the last months of 1869 and at the beginning of 1870 gives us the key to his purposes in the Hohenzollern candidacy for the Spanish throne, for the candidacy was planned to test the reaction of France. Bismarck hoped that the constitutional development of France [toward parliamentary government] would progress and have a tranquilizing effect on Franco-German relations, so that the tension between Prussia and France might be resolved peacefully. He held the constitutional system in France to be "one of the essential means for furthering French development in a peaceful direction and for producing a respect in France for the independence of her neighbors." Yet, in Bismarck's opinion, even a revolutionary development in France could promote a peaceful reorganization of Germany.

On February 24, 1870, one day before Salazar's[1] arrival in Berlin, Bismarck, in a great speech in the Reichstag, rejected the inclusion of Baden in the North German Confederation. Since the political situation forbade him to reveal the true reasons for this decision, he explained his conduct on February 28, 1870, in a detailed dispatch to the Prussian minister in Karlsruhe, who was to bring the contents confidentially to the attention of Prime Minister von Frey-

dorf. Bismarck wished to avoid any discord with the government of Baden. One day earlier, on February 27, he had dictated the first outline of his famous report to the king on the Spanish question, in which he skillfully evaded the essential matter of how the French government would receive the news of the candidacy. The dispatch to Karlsruhe, written under the immediate impression of the offer brought by Salazar, appears now to be an extremely important document. In it can be discerned the actual aims that the chancellor pursued in the Spanish enterprise. Bismarck lists two reasons for his reluctance to incorporate Baden: (1) consideration for the king of Bavaria, upon whose attitude "much depended" in the development of south German relations; (2) consideration for France, whose parliamentary system he wished to spare, since it had "up to this point developed not unsatisfactorily." To Busch[2] he expressed himself similarly: it was important not to subject to another spring frost the constitutional development in France which, "since it promised peace," had been fostered by Berlin in every way. Bismarck said this just after he had begun to promote the candidacy, allegedly with the knowledge that it would cause war, or at least with full awareness that there was danger of war. He continued: "We could carry on a war with France and conquer. Yet four or five [more wars] would ensue, and hence it would be folly, if not a crime, if [what we wish] can be attained by peaceful means. Warlike and revolutionary situations could appear in France that might make more pliable the metal that is now so brittle."

Bismarck steadily rejected the possibility of conjuring up a war as a means

---

[1] Eusebio Salazar y Mazarredo, agent of the Spanish government who conducted the secret negotiations with Bismarck and the Sigmaringen Hohenzollerns that led to Leopold's candidacy for the throne.—*Ed.*

[2] Moritz Busch, press secretary of the German Foreign Office.—*Ed.*

to German unification. He hoped for voluntary union with the south, even if that took many more years. His policy of peaceful unification is all the more important in view of the fact that he was convinced, after conscientious examination of the problem, that Germany would be victorious in such a war. But he was also conscious of the fateful consequences of a military conflict between Germany and France, as his repeated statements right up to the moment of the great decision show. The dispatch to Karlsruhe demonstrates that he expected favorable results from the further development of the parliamentary system in France. Bismarck made it expressly clear to the Baden government that he wished to avoid "recommending at this time a policy that would subject the stability of the system to a hard test." He explained that he had used the Reichstag discussion forced on him by the National Liberals as a means of "accustoming the cabinets and our opponents to the thought that the Peace of Prague does *not* hinder us from completing the unification of Germany." He wanted to approach the partial incorporation [of the south], namely that of Baden and southern Hesse, only when Europe, especially France, had become accustomed to the fact that Prussia was not forbidden by the Peace of Prague from forming a union with either part or the whole of southern Germany; furthermore, he did not want to take steps in this direction until it was apparent whether the constitutional system would succeed or fail in France and until it was possible "in like manner to form a more definite judgment about the future of Bavaria." Still another situation, the dispatch continued, would make possible the incorporation of Baden: the development of a European crisis that

would relieve him of the necessity of cultivating these various conditions favorable to German unity. In conclusion, he again took a position with regard to the question of war: "I am rather free of the concern that we have reason to fear war more than others do; I have complete trust in our ability to conquer if war is forced upon us; but I believe that even a victorious war is a means conscientious governments ought not to employ for the attainment of goals that can doubtless be achieved even without such a step."

After the Luxemburg crisis [of 1867], to be sure, Bismarck counted on the probability of war. That was evident in view of the displacement of power in favor of Prussia-Germany. In addition, the situation was sharpened by domestic conditions in France: Napoleon could not accept a further loss of prestige without severely compromising his position.

The candidacy now offered Bismarck the possibility of creating a crisis in France, thus making "the . . . brittle metal more pliable." France would have been out-maneuvered by the successful fulfillment of his plans. Napoleon would have found himself in circumstances from which there was no escape. Olozaga, the Spanish minister in Paris, appraised the situation correctly when he said that he did not doubt that in certain quarters everything would be done to ruin the Napoleonic dynasty. Bismarck himself declared, "We may witness temporary unrest in France, and we will doubtless have to avoid everything that might bring it about or augment it." Bismarck wanted to weaken Napoleon's position, but in a way that would allow the French nation to accept a *fait accompli* and not compel it under any circumstances to resort to war. If the Prussian state had officially appeared as the challenger, France would have had no other recourse than to pick up the gauntlet. For that reason Bismarck did not wish to be officially involved. The Spaniards were to negotiate directly with Leopold. This tactic would protect the Prussian state and "give it an unassailable position before Europe." "It concerns, on the one hand, a willful act of the Spanish nation and, on the other, of the hereditary prince, who has reached his majority, is the master of his own decisions, and is a private person." France—so Bismarck thought—would undoubtedly raise an alarm, cry "intrigue," and rage at him, but would not find a suitable point of attack. The French counterstroke would only cleave the air. They could be asked, "What do you want? Do you want to dictate the decisions of the Spanish nation and of a German private person?"

If Leopold had only become king of Spain [before the crisis arose], France could hardly have done anything about it. Otherwise it would have had to intervene in the internal affairs of the Spanish nation, for the project would not have involved Prussia in any vulnerable way. France would have had no choice other than to reconcile itself to a *fait accompli*, unless it wished to conduct an aggressive war of doubtful justification on two fronts. Bismarck did not believe Napoleon capable of the kind of aggressive resolution that would have been necessary to launch a counterblow from an almost hopeless situation. By all human calculation, furthermore, such a blow would have had small prospect of success, since he would have found Germany united from the outset. Hence Napoleon would have been compelled to yield peacefully. The French people would have felt their national prestige severely damaged by Bismarck's actions

and, since redress abroad had been cut off, their injured pride would have vented itself against the emperor with probably fatal results. Sooner or later, it would have led to the fall of this constant disturber of European politics. The plan was bold, but not adventurous, for it gave promise of a genuine resolution of the existing friction between Germany and France. The crisis in France would have provided the best moment for solving the German question without foreign intervention. Yet, if war had come, Bismarck would not have had to fear it under these circumstances. If, namely, the French had undertaken a military attack under such unfavorable conditions, there would no longer have been any possibility of a *peaceful* unification of Germany, even by another course. The Bismarck plan was intended to bring about a bloodless solution of the crisis. The chancellor had not acted, moreover, under the belief that war must come sooner or later; on the contrary, he wished to bypass the critical point in order to avoid a war whose further consequences he shunned.

Thus, the candidacy was planned as a *diplomatic* weapon. In accordance with the political methods of that time, war was considered to be an *ultima ratio*. The policy, designed to avoid war, nevertheless passed extremely close to war. The slightest deviation from the steep and narrow path could endanger a peaceful solution. Any uncertain step would have appeared to France as a Prussian weakness, and that would have made war unavoidable. Bismarck had great confidence in his diplomatic artistry. Yet, even if he executed the maneuver skillfully, moments of danger would remain, because a *fait accompli* was the prerequisite for success. Since the election of Leopold as king had to take place before the plan could be put in operation, it was tactically imperative that the action be launched as a complete surprise. That this failed was the consequence of an unfortunate mishap.[3]

One must still ask whether Bismarck did not evaluate certain factors falsely. Long ago [the historian] Rudolf Fester concluded that the scheme was faulty in its basic design. It could only have been successful if the election had been possible without previous announcement. Otherwise, French diplomats would have had eight days in which to react. Whether they could have attained success in this time remains an open question. The weakest point in Bismarck's combination was Spain. The chancellor greatly exaggerated the ability of the Spanish nation to maintain what he conceived to be its honor. He later conceded this himself, and the course of the July crisis of 1870 proved it. He also deceived himself with regard to his king, to whom the ethical and legal aspects of the situation were stronger than political exigencies; through him Bismarck was brought, at the critical moment, almost to the point of defeat.[4] . . .

Bismarck's plan aimed at crippling, if not in fact bypassing, Napoleon's foreign policy, whose restlessness and lack of plan—thrusting first one way, then another—could become dangerous, and which, because of the domestic political pressures exerted upon it, could not concede the unification of Germany. The international political situation was relatively favorable for the blow against the western neighbor. The sequence of moves and countermoves after the appointment of Gramont [as foreign minister] is full of dramatic suspense. While there may be differences of opinion here and there on questions of detail (where in history is that impossible?), there is one fact that I believe to have proved absolutely. Convincing evidence testifies that Bismarck did not want war; the candidacy was not planned to bring about a military solution of the German problem. The chancellor sought a diplomatic defeat of his opponent. Further investigation will show that one cannot speak of a decisive desire for war on France's side. One diplomatic action was opposed by another. Bismarck wanted to weaken the position of Napoleon. When his plan failed, the French attempted to inflict a diplomatic defeat on Prussia. The opponents sought to outmaneuver one another and the war developed out of this excited diplomatic struggle. The cruder the means employed, the more difficult it was to achieve a compromise. In the end the pressure for a solution of the crisis was stronger than the calculating politics of the statesmen.

---

[3] The author is referring to the fact that, owing to a code clerk's error in deciphering a message, the election of Prince Leopold by the Spanish parliament was delayed. During the delay news of the Hohenzollern candidacy reached the public press.—*Ed.*

[4] William I of Prussia, who had to give his consent before his relative, Prince Leopold, could accept the candidacy, was deeply disturbed by the policy urged upon him by Bismarck. Separated from Bismarck while vacationing at Bad Ems, he responded to French pressure by mediating Leopold's renunciation of the throne on July 12. He did reject, however, although courteously, the further demands made upon him by the French through Count Benedetti on July 13. This latter episode, as reported to Berlin in the famous "Ems dispatch" which Bismarck edited and published, was the climactic event that brought about the war.—*Ed.*

LEWIS NAMIER (1888–1960) is chiefly known for
the new techniques he developed for the study of
British political history and applied to the age of
George III. He was also vitally interested in current
politics and in recent European history. During
World War II, when the subject of nationalism was
very much in men's minds, he made a study of its
role in the revolution of 1848. In the essay
from which this selection is taken he analyzes
the revolution as the "seed-plot of history" from
which came the major developments of our age.*

Frankfurt, 1848: Start of
Germany's Bid for World Power

With 1848 starts the German bid for
power, for European predominance, for
world dominion: the national movement
was the common denominator of the
German revolution in 1848, and a
mighty Germany, fit to give the law to
other nations, its foremost aim. *Einheit,
Freiheit, und Macht* ("Unity, Freedom,
and Power") was the slogan, with the
emphasis on the first and third concepts.
"Through power to freedom, this is Germany's predestined path," wrote in April
1848 the outstanding intellectual leader
of the Frankfurt assemblies, Professor
Dahlmann. Even some of the Republicans were Republicans primarily because
they were Nationalists: the existence of
thirty-odd dynasties and the rival claims
of Habsburgs and Hohenzollerns were
the foremost obstacles to German unity,
easiest removed by proclaiming a German Republic, one and indivisible. The
movement for German unity originated
in 1848 in the west, south-west, and in
the centre of Germany, in the small
States which gave no scope to the German *Wille zur Macht*, and in the newly-
acquired, disaffected provinces of Prussia
and Bavaria. But although the aim of the
Frankfurt Parliament was a real Pan-
Germany, not a Great Prussia, or Great
Austria, one of the two German Great
Powers had to be the core of the new
German Federal State. And here started
the difficulties: Austria was the greatest
State within the Federation and its

---

* From *Vanished Supremacies* copyright © Sir Lewis Namier 1958, Hamish Hamilton, London, pp. 28–30.

traditional "head", but of its thirty-six million inhabitants less than six were German; while of sixteen million in Prussia, fourteen were German. Austria obviously could not merge into a German national State, whereas Prussia could—theoretically. It became clear in 1848–1849 that a united Greater Germany (*Gross-Deutschland*), comprising the German provinces of Austria, implied the disruption of Austria; otherwise it had to be a Lesser Germany (*Klein-Deutschland*). With an undivided Austria within Germany, the German Confederation could not change into a Federal State; but a Federation of States offered no prospect of real national unity or of power. The Frankfurt Parliament therefore finished by accepting *Klein-Deutschland*, and offered its Crown to the King of Prussia; who refused from respect for Austria and because he could only have accepted the Crown if offered to him by his fellow-sovereigns. Nor would the new Empire as planned at Frankfurt have proved acceptable to the true Prussians: Frankfurt, not Berlin, was to have been its capital, and Prussia was 'to merge into Germany' (there was intense jealousy at Frankfurt against the Berlin Parliament, and as a safeguard against Prussian predominance in a *Klein-Deutschland* it was planned to break up Prussia into her eight provinces, each about the size of a German middle-sized State). When in March 1848 Frederick William IV sported the German tricolour and made his troops assume it, the Second Regiment of the Guards replied by a song about "the cry which pierced the faithful hearts: you shall be Prussians no longer, you shall be Germans." When Bismarck showed its text to the Prince of Prussia, tears ran down William's cheeks. But it was his system based on Prussia, her army

and administration, which was to be established by the man who showed him the song.

The year 1848 proved in Germany that union could not be achieved through discussion and by agreement; that it could be achieved only by force; that there were not sufficient revolutionary forces in Germany to impose it from below; and that therefore, if it was to be, it had to be imposed by the Prussian army. Again the future was mapped out. There were four programs in 1848–1849. That of *Gross-Oesterreich*, a centralized Germanic Austria retaining her traditional preponderance in Germany, was realized by Schwarzenberg in 1850, after Olmütz. That of a Greater Prussia was realized in the North German Confederation of 1866, and was extended in 1870–1871 to cover the entire territory of the Frankfurt *Klein-Deutschland*. That program itself, with the capital removed from Berlin, was haltingly attempted under the Weimar Republic; while the other Frankfurt program of *Gross-Deutschland*, including the German and Czech provinces of Austria, was achieved by Hitler in 1938–1939.

In 1800, after some forty years in politics, Lord Shelburne wrote in his memoirs:

It requires experience in government to know the immense distance between planning and executing. All the difficulty is with the last. It requires no small labour to open the eyes of either the public or of individuals, but when that is accomplished, you are not got a third of the way. The real difficulty remains in getting people to apply the principles which they have admitted, and of which they are now so fully convinced. Then springs the mine of private interests and personal animosity. . . . If the Emperor Joseph had been content to sow and not to plant, he would have done more good, and saved a great deal of ill.

Most of the men of 1848 lacked political experience, and before a year was out the "trees of liberty" planted by them had withered away. None the less, 1848 remains a seed-plot of history. It crystallized ideas and projected the pattern of things to come; it determined the course of the century which followed. It planned, and its schemes have been realized: but—*non vi si pensa quanto sangue costa.*

FRANZ SCHNABEL (1887–1966) is chiefly known as
the erudite author of a scholarly four-volume history
of early nineteenth-century Germany, a work that
parallels the classic study of Heinrich von
Treitschke. Unlike Treitschke, Schnabel is critical
of aspects of the German tradition; the creation of
a nation-state was not for him the principal goal of
German history. In this address, delivered before
a meeting of French and German historians in 1949,
he subjects Bismarck's aims in foreign policy to
a new and searching criticism. His analysis produced
sharp responses from several leading German
historians, among them Gerhard Ritter,
whose arguments appear in the next selection.*

► *Federalism Preferable*
to a National State

My topic, while of intellectual and historical interest, also has great significance for the present. It ought to contribute to the establishment of a new European order and give foreigners an understanding of Bismarck's personality and his place in his times.

My point of departure is the current view, usually found in Germany today, which regards Bismarck as a great statesman in foreign affairs but one whose domestic policy was inadequate. According to this view, he had many of the shortcomings of his social class; he had no idea how to draw the people and the parties into sharing responsibility; he did not understand the importance of

the Fourth Estate and as a consequence he intentionally made the workers into dependents of the state while refusing them the freedom to organize and the right to participate in governing it. Furthermore, he threw many priests into jail, something which had not happened in Europe since the time of the Jacobins. Hence the general opinion today is that Bismarck made a great many errors in domestic policy.

On the other hand it is maintained that Bismarck was never equalled as a diplomat and foreign minister, that he employed the methods of diplomacy with great finesse, and that his was the only possible solution to the German question

* From Franz Schnabel, "Bismarck und die Nationen," *Europa und der Nationalismus,
Bericht über das III internationale Historiker-Treffen in Speyer—17 bis 20, Oktober 1949* (Baden-Baden: Verlag für Kunst und Wissenschaft, 1950), pp. 91–108, translated by Otto Pflanze. By permission of Verlag für Kunst und Wissenschaft.

at that time. The brilliant portraits of Bismarck that uncritical biographers such as Erich Marcks and A. O. Meyer painted have become tarnished. But attempts are being made to preserve at least the diplomatic side of his career in its former luster.

Bismarck's admirers could always point to the fact that, if nothing else, he was obviously successful. Experience has repeatedly shown, however, that in history, as in personal life, only a much later epoch can decide conclusively what constitutes success. Bismarck's Reich lasted only fifty years.

Today the causes of this failure are sought primarily in the constitution Bismarck gave the Reich and in the spirit in which it was administered. With regard to foreign policy, however, it is said that the mistakes of his successors (figures of "Wilhelmian stamp" from Chancellor Bülow down to Reichstag deputies like Ernst Bassermann) were responsible for the development that led to the collapse of 1918. In no way can the statesman Bismarck be held responsible for Germany's fate in the twentieth century. At most he shares the responsibility in that he failed to train a new generation of diplomats.

This is essentially the common opinion of Bismarck today, and it is most cogently expressed by Hans Rothfels. In his early works Rothfels voiced sharp criticism of Bismarck's domestic policy, especially his social policy. On the basis of documents from the archives he proved that Bismarck simply ignored the advice of his counselors in the field of social policy in building up the German system of social security. He made the workers recipients of state aid with the object of giving them an interest in the Reich. Yet as Rothfels shows in his biography of Theodor Lohmann, his

counselors, especially Lohmann, warned him that he would achieve nothing more than conversion of the workers into petty bourgeois—Philistines who would be amenable to the wishes of anyone who came to power. In his essays, reviews, and speeches, however Rothfels has extolled Bismarck as the master of foreign policy, defending him against all attacks and seeking to prove that Bismarck's policies, meaning both his goals and his methods, were the only ones possible in the nineteenth century.

Other historians have recently held, however, that foreign and domestic policy can hardly be considered apart from one another. Contrary to previous opinion, Bismarck's foreign policy was inevitably handicapped by the fact that the man who created the Reich remained so limited by the prejudices of his class and so engrossed in a drive for power. Hence the views of the liberals of the 1860s have been revived, according to which a liberal constitution and liberal legislation would not only have strengthened the Reich in foreign affairs but would have made unnecessary the Machiavellian methods that Bismarck employed. This is the central thesis in the great work of Erich Eyck, to whom we are indebted for what is still the best biography of Bismarck. According to Eyck, those methods would have been unnecessary if the liberals had founded the Reich, because the liberals would have inspired more confidence in Germany and throughout the world. Friedrich Meinecke also inclines to this opinion.

In all of these explanations and discussions Bismarck's work—the creation of a compact national state in the heart of Europe—has never been exposed to discussion or challenge. When his foreign policy is attacked, it is on the basis that he did not hesitate to use the most extreme means. For he intentionally produced three wars and was proud of the fact that he had driven princes from their thrones, and that he was the first to say that he would not stumble over legal obstacles. He did not avoid intrigue but was never more than a dilettante in this art. Certainly it was very clumsy of him to pretend in 1870 that he knew nothing about the Spanish throne candidacy and to act as though it did not involve him and the king (at least, in his role as king). Likewise his negotiations with Cardinal Jacobini, papal secretary of state, over the Septennate Law inevitably failed for the same reason.[1]

If the Bismarck problem is to be conceived correctly, it is above all necessary to determine whether Bismarck's achievements and his methods can be separated from one another and whether the Reich could actually have been founded in the middle of the last century by other means. Further, it is necessary to subject his achievements as such to another historical examination. Until now this has not been done and, as long as it is not done, we can neither get an accurate picture of Bismarck nor place his personality and achievements in their proper historical context.

Let us examine first Bismarck's methods or, to put it briefly, his Machiavellism. Machiavellian politics are certainly not merely a supplement to and an attendant phenomenon of the modern state; they are a necessary

[1] In 1887 the Catholic Center party voted against the German army appropriation bill (Septennate). Despite the fact that Bismarck succeeded through Jacobini, in getting the Pope to disapprove of this action in the public press, the Center party succeeded in maintaining its parliamentary strength in the election of that year.—Ed.

consequence of the collapse of medieval unity. As soon as there were many powers seeking to round off their frontiers, to expand and conquer, and as soon as it became necessary in the interest of their security to maintain the European balance of power, it was only natural that such methods should appear. Through use, they were developed to a fine art. This development began in Italy, where the idea of the balance of power first appeared, and then spread throughout Europe. The naturalistic spirit of the Italian Renaissance, which demanded that one follow only the dictates of nature, simply gave the theoretical justification and direction for this policy. We do not know whether Moritz of Saxony read Machiavelli, but he acted according to Machiavelli's precepts in striving for power and expansion. Thomas More, the chancellor of Henry VIII, did read Machiavelli, and he too sought to create a compact state. Nor is it true that in modern times there have been no tributary peoples. The fate of the Irish may be an exception, but it is notable that, although their tributary status was for the most part established through the absolutism of Henry VIII and Oliver Cromwell, they were able to liberate themselves from the status of a colonial people only after a long struggle against an aristocratic political order. Throughout the centuries of the monarchical period it was the same—from Richelieu to Frederick the Great, Talleyrand, Cavour, and Bismarck. I have excluded Kaunitz and Metternich because the Hapsburgs of that time were already on the political defensive among the European powers. The ambitious states of those centuries wanted first the balance of power, then hegemony, a fullness of power, and a compact state. The methods for achieving these ends were the methods of the old, classical diplomacy, and these were developed with the greatest skill. The first was the statistical method, which consisted in accumulating provinces, rounding off the frontiers of the state, balancing off other states, and discovering combinations or alliances. Associated with the statistical method was that of computation, which estimated, according to the laws of probability, the likely behavior of the opponent in view of the general situation and the possible course of events. They dealt with more or less known quantities: with certain states whose vital interests and whose *raison d'état* had to be studied, and with personalities such as kings, ministers, and favorites whom they sought to understand with the help of psychology. Certainly there was much that was beyond calculation. But in general men acted according to their interests and only seldom did the monarch of a great power pay no attention to *raison d'état*. Hence it was possible to calculate how another ruler would react by discerning his interests as well as those of his state. In this way practical politics were conducted according to the precepts of Machiavelli. This kind of diplomacy is revealed in many records that document the classical spirit; consider, for example, the state papers of Talleyrand or Metternich.

Bismarck was the last great master of this kind of diplomacy. We know much more about him, however, than about the earlier statesmen because less of the evidence has been destroyed; for that reason it is easier to take note of all his sins. Bismarck's case is also different in that he was an outsider in his profession, having come to diplomacy late in his career by way of parliament. Student

fraternity, officers' club, and parliament provided his only schooling for diplomacy. For him, at least it was hardly the best preparation. He did not learn self-restraint. In contrast to Talleyrand, who said that words exist only in order to conceal thoughts, Bismarck did not hesitate to speak his mind. He enjoyed indulging his inclination for satire and irony, with the consequence that his recorded cynicisms are numerous. Finally it must be remembered that the world was changing rapidly during his time and was no longer as calculable as it had been. The great change was that the cabinets no longer led the people but the people the cabinets, and this introduced an element into politics that was beyond all calculation. As long as Bismarck had to deal only with the court in Petersburg, the old methods sufficed. But the emergence of Pan-Slavism brought classical diplomacy to an end.

As nationalism was further advanced and became completely imbued with the new concept of the state, it too followed the precepts of Machiavelli. The difference was that nationalism strove for a compact nation rather than for a compact state. Democracies can also practice Machiavellism in foreign policy, and it is valid to conclude that the German liberals could have created the German national state only through constant contest with the great powers. It was the liberals who demanded the return of Alsace-Lorraine and of Schleswig-Holstein. Although their justification was different, this was also a kind of "reunion" policy.[2] The liberals too were in agreement with the theft of Hanover.

[2] The author is referring to the "courts of reunion" through which Louis XIV of France acquired parts of Lorraine from the Holy Roman Empire.—*Ed.*

But they did not understand how to carry out their policies with the versatility of a Bismarck in utilizing all opportunities, and it is doubtful whether they would have reached the goal.

For these reasons it is false to criticize Bismarck's methods while accepting his goal; namely, the creation of a large compact state in the heart of Europe, whether organized on a federal or centralistic basis. This goal could not be attained by other means. It was the goal that nationalists everywhere set for themselves as soon as they accepted the idea of a compact state and applied it to the nation. This was true among the Italians, the Czechs, the Hungarians, the Poles, and the southern Slavs. Yet we must question whether this was the only way in which Europe could have been reorganized in the middle of the nineteenth century. The issue is whether Bismarck had to make a decision and whether there was any viable alternative.

Let us reconstruct the situation with which Bismarck was confronted. At the Congress of Vienna in 1815 classical diplomacy in the old style carried the day, specifically the statistical statecraft of the balance of power in its pure form. The diplomats were directed to redivide the world according to number rather than kind. Patriots of all nations (Stein, Confalonieri, Szechenyi). remained in the antechamber. One nation alone refused to be satisfied with this: the Norwegians did not let themselves be "bartered away like cattle." The actual content of the political history of the nineteenth century is the contest of peoples against the settlement of the Congress of Vienna and the dissolution of that settlement. In the beginning there was no talk of the compact national state. German patriots were still thinking of the old Empire; national sentiment was

not yet awake in the East; and neither the concepts of the French Revolution nor those of German romanticism had become a power in the East. The Prussian reformers began the regeneration of their state with the idea that it must surpass the rest of Germany in three areas: arms, constitutionalism, and intellectual attainment (that is, through "moral conquests"). But Stein and Arndt[3] held to the old Empire and were convinced that political leadership was Austria's role. No one was more critical than Arndt of Frederick the Great and the old mechanistic statecraft and diplomacy. For that reason he wished to reform the Prussian state.

The idea of the compact national state appeared in German life in the 1840s in two forms: the *grossdeutsch* republic and the *kleindeutsch* or Prussian, hereditary empire. The idea of a *grossdeutsch* republic failed. The conception could not be realized, for in 1849 the *grossdeutsch* republicans compromised themselves by coming to terms with those who advocated a hereditary empire. Their revolution was defeated and their leaders emigrated.

The second form of the idea, which sought creation of a *kleindeutsch* national state under Prussian leadership, also emerged in the 1840s. This is the type that Bismarck achieved. He stemmed from the old system of statecraft and he sought through its methods to expand and round off the borders of a greater Prussian state. This objective led him naturally to the *kleindeutsch* national idea.

The conception of the *kleindeutsch* national state (and of the Bismarck Reich, whose historical significance we

[3] Ernst Moritz Arndt was a patriotic poet who helped to mobilize German public opinion for the struggle against Napoleon I.—*Ed*

are examining) did not have a long period of preparation. It developed very quickly and was transformed into reality through Bismarck's policies. Its history comprised three stages. The idea of Prussian leadership, although still connected with the old imperial idea and with the romantic doctrine of nationality (*Volkstum*), appeared first. This was followed by a desire for a greater Prussia produced by the reawakening of the Frederician tradition, which had almost become extinct during the period of the Restoration. Finally, the two ideas were united—the idea of a nation led by Prussia and the idea of a compact great-Prussian state. At this point the idea of a *kleindeutsch* national state was born.

Let us now examine the first stage. The idea of Prussian leadership appeared first in connection with the *grossdeutsch* and romantic-national ideals. It was introduced into literature by *Turnvater* Jahn.[4] An ardent romanticist, Jahn accepted the doctrine of the national spirit (*Volksgeist*); he was the first to employ the concept of "*Volkstum*." He was deeply influenced by the ideas of Rousseau and, if he failed to become the German Rousseau, his arbitrariness and abstruse style were responsible. Jahn rejected Austria as a "jumble of people" ("*Völkermang*"). In his view the national state should embrace all "members of the Empire," all adherents of German *Volkstum*. Hence Jahn came to the idea of a central state under Prussian leadership and including Switzerland, Holland, and Austria. It was a purely literary conception. The idea of Prussian leadership came closer to reality for the first time during the struggle over

Saxony,[5] when it was developed by Gneisenau, Niebuhr, and Arndt. Whatever strengthens Prussia, they said, is a step toward German unity. This was the essence of the Prussian view of history. In this view, nevertheless, Prussian leadership was still associated with the *grossdeutsch* form—"*Soweit die deutsche Zunge klingt!*" ("Where'er is heard the German tongue!")[6]

The second stage, the concept of Prussian leadership in a great Prussian, or *kleindeutsch*, state, could only be conceived on Prussian soil. In a letter of 1814 Ludwig von der Marwitz[7] wrote to Hardenberg that Prussia must take over the now compelling idea of a common German fatherland, and must realize this idea step by step, seizing any favorable opportunity to incorporate neighboring regions. There was no talk here of moral conquests, or of any Prussian service to the nation, but only of purely Prussian interests. This is entirely *kleindeutsch* and entirely Bismarckian, at least in so far as the period of the founding of the Reich is concerned. For a while, however, the idea had no following and the passage from Marwitz's papers is a mere curiosity. The patriotic upsurge of 1813–1814 quickly subsided; soon the ideal of a common fatherland seemed to be replaced by the Holy Alliance and stability. From the viewpoint of the nobility, this was as it should be. Ludwig von Gerlach stressed that Prussia, unlike France and England, did not have a mission to become a compact monarchy. For the most varied reasons the Junkers

---

[4] Friedrich Ludwig Jahn founded a movement of gymnastic clubs (*Turnvereine*) which propagated national patriotism during the War of Liberation against Napoleon I.—*Ed.*

[5] In 1814 one of the chief issues at the Congress of Vienna concerned Prussia's desire to annex the kingdom of Saxony.—*Ed.*

[6] From a patriotic poem, "The German's Fatherland," composed by Arndt.—*Ed.*

[7] Ludwig von der Marwitz was the leader of the conservative opposition to the Prussian reforms of 1807–1819.—*Ed.*

were opposed to the continuation of the general reform of the state, and under no condition did they wish to see a compact unity formed out of the nine parts of the monarchy. Yet the task of reform was now urgent. Although the chancellor, Prince Hardenberg, and the bureaucracy undertook it again, they were handicapped by the general fear of revolution and by the spirit of the Restoration. In the alliance between king, nobility, and bureaucracy the latter was the weakest party. Hardenberg put through a reorganization of the administration, but no central diet was formed, only provincial diets. All further attempts at a unitary reform were blocked.

In only one area was unification unavoidable, chiefly because it coincided with the interests of the nobility. This was the customs union (Zollverein) created by Friedrich Motz. He was a member of the bureaucracy but, having immigrated from Hesse, was not a Prussian. For that reason he could become the partisan of both greater Prussia and the German nation. As evidenced in his famous memoradum of 1829, Motz was the first to combine the idea of Prussian leadership with that of the political expansion of Prussia over the whole of *Kleindeutschland*. His conception remained alive in the Zollverein; it lived on in Bismarck and Rudolf Delbrück.[8] They kept Austria out of the Zollverein although economic reasons favored its inclusion. If in the course of this address Bismarck's intervention is found responsible for the fact that a *kleindeutsch* Reich, was created rather than a [federalized] central Europe, we must keep in mind that he had forerunners in

[8] Rudolf Delbrück was the Prussian official chiefly responsible for economic affairs and hence in charge of the negotiations that led to the reconstruction of the German Zollverein on a free-trade basis in the 1860s.—*Ed.*

Motz and Delbrück. Economic interests alone held the Zollverein together; yet "a Zollverein is not a fatherland." Dislike for the Prussian Zollverein by Germans in the south and along the Rhine was great, and economic necessity alone forced them to enter it. The Zollverein could be converted into a lasting political union only if Prussia became constitutional; that is, if Prussia made "moral conquests."

The third stage was to create a *kleindeutsch* Reich by bringing Prussia into harmony with the constitutional south and the liberal west. It is notable that a Rhenish businessman, Friedrich Daniel Bassermann, was the first to propose the creation of a German parliament at a German political convention in 1844. While tradesmen, manufacturers, and early industrialists did not think merely of economic interests, it was the intellectuals who undertook the task of synthesizing Prussianism, Protestanism, and German freedom and who, as a consequence, completed the *kleindeutsch* idea. The first was Johann Gustav Droysen, who expressed the idea, with complete clarity as to its goal, in his lectures of 1842 on the wars of liberation. It is understandable that Metternich supported the conservatives in Prussia and that Bavaria was happy that Prussia was ruled by reactionaries.

Seldom in history has an idea had such a short career as that of the *kleindeutsch* national state. There was hardly any talk of it in 1840; yet the victory of the *Kleindeutschen* came as early as 1848–1849. To be sure, Frederick William IV rejected their program for a Reich constitution; but he immediately took up the idea and with the aid of Radowitz sought to achieve their aim through negotiations with the princes. He concluded the League of Three Kings with

Saxony and Hanover and presented his constitutional draft to the *kleindeutsch* party in Gotha. At this moment Prussian troops stood in the Bavarian Palatinate and in Baden; the princes were dependent on their support in the struggle against the revolution; and the chances for Prussia were most favorable. Everything dependent on whether Bavaria would join this alliance, and here Radowitz met opposition. Minister-President von der Pfordten, who was from new Bavaria (Franconia) and a Protestant, rejected the entire plan for the German Union. His memoranda on the subject reveal how well he foresaw the harm that Bismarck's ideas would cause. He objected to the *kleindeutsch* concept as such, not only from the standpoint of Bavarian but also of German and European politics. The hereditary hegemony of Prussia would, he remarked, lead to Germany's dismemberment, for Austria would become a Slavic state with a German dependency and *Kleindeutschland* would be politically powerless against Russia and the Slavic peoples. The rich regions in the East, Pfordten continued, would be closed to Germany if they were no longer ruled by Vienna. And if Austria were to separate itself from Germany, a centralistic government would be unavoidable for *Kleindeutschland*. Furthermore, this *kleindeutsch* Reich would have a powerful attraction for the Austrian Germans and would bring about a movement for union with it. The separation of Austria from Germany would be harmful to both parties, for Austria would be robbed of its German character. The position of the German nation in Europe would come to be untenable and result in a partition similar to that of Poland. There can be no doubt that Radowitz was a forerunner of Bismarck, but **Bismarck** did

not come to this policy of expansion until 1859.

In 1859 Bismarck's position on the subject of the nations became clear. This year was of greatest importance, for it saw the beginning of a new world epoch. Nationalism commenced to revolutionize the old order first in central Europe and then in eastern Europe. In 1859 two national states were conceived in central Europe, from which the principle of the national state spread to eastern Europe. But its triumph in the latter region finally brought about the collapse of central Europe. As stated earlier, the fact that the peoples of Europe dissolved the settlement of the Congress of Vienna was the basic theme of the nineteenth century. The dissolution had already begun during the Crimean War, when the struggle between Austria and Russia brought about the collapse of the Holy Alliance. This destroyed the old state system, and the powers themselves were responsible. What was to take its place? Italy answered this question immediately, in 1859. In that year a divided nation rose, cast off alien rule, and created a compact state. It was achieved by a legitimate dynasty and with Machiavellian means by two shrewd operators, Victor Emanuel and Cavour. In accordance with its origin there now appeared a monarchy based on a revolutionary foundation with a court lacking an old nobility, a parliament lacking a house of lords, and a regime under the ban of the church. In a Catholic country the monarchy was dependent on radicals and socialists; its parliamentary system was quite different from that of England. This new monarchy was basically nothing more than a façade, a monarchy that clung to the coattails of Jacobinism and later of Mussolini.

The revival of France, furthermore,

occurred in connection with the rise of the House of Savoy. The year 1859 compares with 1796, when Bonaparte stood in northern Italy at the head of a French army poised for an all-out attack against Austria.

This event forced the *kleindeutsch* party to decide whether France or Austria was the "hereditary enemy." Previously *kleindeutsch* historians had always directed their arrows at both—condemning both France's "lust for the Rhine" and the "fatal" role of the House of Hapsburg. Now a decision had to be made. It is well known that public opinion and the Prince Regent chose sides against France but demanded concessions from Austria in the "German question." This was in accord with the policy of creating a compact national state. Yet France and Austria forestalled the Prussian action by reaching a settlement.

What everybody—liberals and nationalists, Prince Regent and Bismarck—had in common was the plan to create a compact national state in central Europe. They differed from one another only with regard to the means to that end. It is notable that at this time the traditional system of politics and diplomacy was subjected by Constantin Frantz to a searching criticism on the grounds that times had greatly changed and new ways had to be sought. Like Minister von der Pfordten earlier, Frantz rejected in advance Bismarck's solution for the founding of the Reich. A Prussian by birth, he was the son of a cleric and an official in the Prussian service until Russian pressure forced his resignation. Friendship with Russia was the cornerstone of Prussian policy; yet he warned the *kleindeutsch* architects about Russia.

Like Bismarck, Constantin Frantz argued, from facts that were indisputable. The European balance of power

was dead, as was the Holy Alliance, and Russia's ascendancy was obviously imminent despite her defeat in the Crimean War! Russia's entry into European history was certainly the greatest event of the nineteenth century. Russia attempted four times to push into the Balkans (1811, 1824, 1828, 1877), but on each occasion had to retreat, chiefly because Austria was still a great power after 1815. World War I began precisely over the question of domination of the critical areas in the Balkans. Yet despite these facts the Prussian government clung to Russia during the nineteenth century and with the help of Sardinia, attempted to force Austria out of Germany. Russia's goal in the future was unmistakable: to found a world empire whose borders would lie on the Elbe and on the line from Hamburg to Trieste. This is what Constantin Frantz foresaw in 1859.

The second fact was the ascendancy of France to a position of world power. In 1859 France had a powerful army and its government was concentrated in the hands of one person. France had troops in Rome, had made great progress in the Orient, had achieved success in China, and was reaching out toward North America.

The European balance of power was already at an end in 1859, for the European great powers were overshadowed by two states that were on the way to becoming world powers. A European balance of power was no longer possible, since it depended on the existence of several great powers. "The concept of the great power belongs to the past, and in future its place will be taken by world powers." This concept of "world power," which belonged to the future, was coined by Constantin Frantz in 1859. But what is understood by the term "world power"? First, such a power had to have a powerful navy, in order to bring pressure on alien coasts. Secondly, it had to have a territorial basis of sufficient size to enable the state to exert a natural influence on distant continents. And third, it must possess a unique political and philosophical outlook capable of being propagated. Russia had all three of these prerequisites, as did the United States, for the latter was to surmount even the difficulties of the Civil War. England, on the other hand, was an artificial world power, for it lacked the territorial basis. France wanted to become a world power, but it could scarcely expect to establish itself in Mexico and in the Sudan. Thus Constantin Frantz predicted the two world powers of the future: Russia and the United States. As far as the present was concerned, he pointed to Russia and France, which flanked central Europe. Considered from this standpoint, the *kleindeutsch* project was senseless, since such a Reich would be much too weak to assert itself in the world struggle of the future. That was his thesis. He stressed that one must clearly understand that neither Prussia nor Austria could exist alone, and that the whole of central Europe must be brought together if a new Balkans was not to come into existence. One must think, moreover, about those other countries, such as Scandinavia, whose vital interests were threatened by Russia. Frantz also considered the non-Russian Slavs, who were as yet untouched by the literature and outlook of Pan-Slavism.

This was the only conception seriously put forward in opposition to Bismarck. What ought to be created in central Europe was not a compact national state, but a federation based on vital popular forces and ethnic and tribal groups (*Volksstämme*). We know that Con-

stantin Frantz developed and justified his proposal for a federal system on many grounds. It sprang from his analysis of the world situation and from the organic viewpoint characteristic of German thought. It was a peculiarity of the German nation that it still possessed tribal groups (*Volksstämme*). They had been split up, to be sure, with the rise of principalities toward the end of the Middle Ages. Yet the formation of large territorial states based on the old tribes began during the Reformation. [These states, Frantz believed, could become the foundation for a federal union of Central Europe.]

Constantin Frantz and Bismarck belonged to two different worlds. It would be a distortion to place the political writer on the same plane with the man responsible for the direction of a great European power. German and Austrian statesmen, especially those who were involved in the Frankfurt Congress of Princes,[9] have recorded in numerous memoranda what could be said against Bismarck. There can be no doubt that Bismarck's concēption was the more limited one, being restricted to Prussia, *Kleindeutschland,* and to the continent. Nor can it be denied that Bismarck's only concern was the attainment of his immediate goal; this was for him the essence and virtue of "state policy." There can also be no question but that things have developed as Bismarck's critics predicted. It is said that Bismarck cannot be measured according to the world situation of 1918 or 1945; yet the

[9] In August 1863 Emperor Franz Joseph proposed a federal reorganization of the German Confederation on a pattern favorable to Austrian interests. Yielding to Bismarck's strenuous objection, William I refused to attend a Congress of Princes which assembled at Frankfurt-on-the-Main to consider the proposal. His absence caused the plan to collapse.—*Ed.*

fact remains that the world situation was fully apparent at that time. The chance for a central European solution was just as evident in German life as was the chance for a *kleindeutsch* solution. Bismarck's intervention was decisive. He rejected all hints of the coming world situation and united Prussian power politics with the *kleindeutsch* program in foreign policy. He was too wise not to recognize that the criticism contained some truth, yet the entire problem was too complicated; it was too remote from his accustomed viewpoint, his pattern of thought, and his background and education. When pressed, he left everything to his Lord and Master in accord with his pietistic outlook: "Everything human is only provisional." This is true, but it ought not to frustrate a far-seeing policy. Bismarck had no conception of a world-embracing Christianity; he was aware only of his king, his fellow nobility, and his Prussian state. He was conservative, but he also renewed the Frederician style of statecraft. He gave to German and to European history a very special course.

The Bismarck Reich, the compact national state under Prussian leadership, had only a short historical preparation. It was a completely unhistorical conception in German life. It had no roots in the people. Before Bismarck's appearance, moreover, the Frederician tradition had become nearly extinct. All possibilities were still open. Then the man appeared who gave to German affairs a direction which, after all that has happened, we must characterize as fateful. The creation of such a national state was only possible because the barriers in the east, which had been erected by Prince Eugene, were weakened; because a lasting alliance was concluded between Prussia and Russia against Austria; and because the existence of the Reich was based upon the methods of the old monarchy, upon transitory alliances, upon competitive armaments, upon the systematic increase of the state income, upon the methods of classical diplomacy, and hence upon militarism, capitalism, and Machiavellism. This is the course which Bismarck took and never left. The methods he employed were indispensable because the goal remained the same.

One cannot condemn the methods Bismarck used if one regards his work as necessary. He was the last talented master of the old statecraft. But the times and the situation required new ways. No one is obliged to do more than he can. Yet Bismarck became through his skill and will power the first man of his age. His decision determined what was to come.

A scholar of wide range and great productivity,
GERHARD RITTER (1888–1967) has written,
among other works, biographies of Martin Luther,
Frederick the Great, and Baron vom Stein. His most
significant work on recent German history is a
three-volume study of German militarism from the
eighteenth to the twentieth centuries. In the essays
from which this selection is taken, Ritter draws
on his knowledge and impressions of the Bismarck
period to rebut what he calls the "surprising"
thesis of Schnabel. The debate is indicative of the
perseverance in historical writing of the
grossdeutsch-kleindeutsch issue that bitterly divided
the revolutionaries of 1848.*

National State More Realistic than Federalism

The problem of interpreting Bismarck in our day has grown from the attempts to persuade the German people that their national hero was in fact a false god like Adolf Hitler, that the renowned founder of the Reich was in truth the author of our political misfortune. Since 1945 a veritable deluge of articles has appeared on this theme—a literature which is often characterized more by its political zeal than by its historical competency. Has this public "revaluation of all values" been successful?

Those who limit themselves to literary sources of this kind could well believe it. Until now, contrary opinions have hardly been ventured. Of course not. For even today the political current is still powerful enough to ostracize anyone who contradicts it. He who does not think "with the times" is "reactionary." To be reactionary has had since 1789 a connotation of moral opprobrium. Who wants to jeopardize his political reputation by defending a great man who has long since passed into history? In particular, who would want to do this when, as in the case of Bismarck, the reproach of callous "nationalism" is combined with that of reaction?

Yet the outpourings from the press are deceptive. There can be no doubt that, beneath the surface, veneration of Bismarck has by no means come to an end in Germany, and that it may even be on the increase. The very radicalism

* From Gerhard Ritter, "Das Bismarckproblem," *Merkur*, vol. 4 (1950), pp. 657–664, translated by Otto Pflanze. By permission of the author.

of the attacks on him arouses contradiction. It appears to me a serious danger that this will actually lead to a hardened nationalism. Is this surprising? Bismarck's name is inseparably associated with the most fortunate period of political and economic ascent in German history, a history so rich in misfortunes. Can anyone expect that a people, as long as it does not despair of itself, should permit even this memory to be condemned as unwholesome?

It is always the historical-political half-truths that do the greatest damage. Of course there is need today for a fundamental revision of the traditional picture of Bismarck. Of course there are political traditions of the Bismarck period that have had an unhealthy influence and whose dangerous one-sidedness must be exposed. But whoever embarks on such a task cannot proceed too carefully and conscientiously if he really wishes to be convincing. Iconoclasm is easy, but it only arouses bitter opposition. It does not enlighten; it confuses.

The history of professional German biographies of Bismarck can only be described as unfortunate. What was written before World War I still lay under the shadow of the great man himself, whose *Realpolitik*, at least in diplomatic questions, was credited with near infallibility. After the collapse of 1918 the distance had become greater and research on Bismarck soon became lively. Sources were assembled and published on a massive basis; thousands of individual questions were clarified; the general outlook and political views of the great *Machtpolitiker* were established much more firmly than before. Yet German historiography did not achieve a great, comprehensive biography before the appearance of the Hitler Reich. One had been expected from Erich Marks since 1909, but his first volume did not get

beyond the year 1848. Instead, he published in 1936 his history of Germany, 1807–1878, in which Bismarck played the leading role—an artistically written work of his old age that never became really popular. That none of the younger researchers took up the task before 1933 must be explained entirely on technical grounds; after that date political considerations were an additional factor. In the Hitler period it was undertaken by only one professional German historian, A. O. Meyer, who during World War II wrote a character sketch that grew into a political biography. It was the work of an enthusiastic venerator of Bismarck who had dedicated his entire life to a succession of studies on the theme and was more at home in the Bismarck family archives than any other scholar. In many of the book's formulations one can detect the attitude of inner protest of an Old Prussian conservative against Hitlerism. But the author, who died in an accident in 1944, did not live to see its appearance; the entire edition was burned as a result of aerial bombardment. It was reprinted, but its appearance was delayed for political reasons. Not until 1950 did it appear on the markets, with a critical foreward by Hans Rothfels.

Meanwhile, the first great biography of Bismarck based on scientific research and a critical examination of the sources had already appeared outside Germany. This was the study by an outsider and emigrant, the former lawyer Erich Eyck. Within Germany it gradually became known after 1945. Abroad, it appears to be the basis for the world's present concept of Bismarck. The two authors, Meyer and Eyck, did not know each other, but, one book reads like a refutation of the other. Every discussion of the Bismarck problem moves between these poles.

It can truthfully be said that both of these works have political orientations which no longer correspond to the issues of our times. Meyer's monarchism and "German-national" conservatism are just as antiquated as the leftist liberalism, in the style of Eugen Richter and Ludwig Bamberger, that Eyck still unreservedly represents today. Eyck's book can be called a delayed revenge of the German liberals of 1862–1866 who were overwhelmed and corrupted by Bismarck —this is even its primary political service! On the other hand, the work of Meyer sounds like a final echo of the thought of the generation that received its earliest political impressions on pilgrimages to Friedrichsruh and studied Bismarck's memoirs as the first source of its political education. Meyer's book was written with warm, at times almost sentimental, affection. Eyck displays admiration for Bismarck's genius but a deep distaste for his politics that increases steadily from the first to the third volume and finally reaches the point of open hatred. Both love and hate can illuminate, but can also blind. We shall have to seek our own way between them.

Recently an attack on the Bismarck problem has come from still a third direction, from the Munich historian Franz Schnabel. To Schnabel the issue is not Bismarck's political methods but his goal, the foundation of a *kleindeutsch* Reich. His critique, which is brilliantly formulated and expressed with considerable spirit, must concern us first because it deals with the most fundamental issues.[1]

In judging Bismarck's politics, professional historians have long been accustomed to distinguish between the diplomat and the statesman of domestic affairs. The old protest of the liberals against the policy of "blood and iron" gradually faded after the brilliant victories of 1866 and 1870–1871. On the other hand, criticism of Bismarck's autocratic leadership, his treatment of political parties, and his general conduct in domestic politics has always remained lively. Since 1919 it has increased considerably. Today this distinction, between domestic and foreign policy, is no longer regarded as valid, as all the earlier indictments of Bismarck's foreign policy have once more come to life. Erich Eyck has renewed the complaints of the liberals during the period of the constitutional conflict against Bismarck as the brutal Machiavelli and violator of the law. Against the dynastic and military victory of Prussian hegemony in Germany he opposes the old concept of "moral conquests," which trusts in the irresistible attraction of national and liberal ideals and in the sweep of popular currents. Schnabel's criticism goes still further; it is directed against Bismarck's entire life's work. "The compact national state under Prussian leadership," he thinks, was not only a "completely unhistorical conception" without root in the people, but it has "given a fateful direction to German affairs." In contrast, he describes what he wishes Bismarck had founded—not a *grossdeutsch,* but a central European federation, a league of states which (if I understand him correctly) would have united all nationalities living in the region of central Europe, including both the German Confederation and Austria-Hungary, against the "flanking powers" of Russia and France. The founding of such a state, which could have built upon the concept of the medieval Reich, would, in Schnabel's opinion, have of-

[1] Some of the passages quoted by the author in the following paragraphs are from another article by Schnabel, the English translation of which is "The Bismarck Problem," in Hans Kohn, ed., *German History: Some New German Views* (London, 1954), pp. 65–93.—*Ed.*

fered a double advantage. First, it would have prevented the movement for national states—which has proved to be an unhealthy and destructive force in Europe in the twentieth century—from penetrating into the east and southeast from the center of the continent and producing "chaos" there, particularly in the area of the Danube. Secondly, it would have created a great central European political structure which would have been much more capable than *Kleindeutschland* of withstanding the pressure of the flanking European powers, Russia and France, the two growing world powers of the nineteenth century whose dualism has been replaced in our times by that of Russia and the United States.

Schnabel declares that such a basic reexamination of Bismarck's work has "not occurred until now." His thesis is indeed surprising. Surprising above all is the challenging statement that Bismarck should have departed from the system of "free competition among national states on the basis of self interest," which has existed since the beginning of modern times (only since then?) and have pursued instead a universal policy which would have "based the communal life of men and peoples upon Christian principles." Instead of carrying on power politics he should have "brought the state back to its original purpose, namely that of helping to realize the good, the right, the higher order." But can there be a realization of "higher orders," a securing of the right, without power? Was there in the international world of the nineteenth century any practical way to execute a successful policy without taking into account the "free competition among national states on the basis of self interest" (which, on the contrary, ruled the whole world and still governs

it to this day); that is, without *raison d'état* in the traditional sense of the phrase? When examined more closely, Schnabel's criticism proves to be a modernized version of the ideas of Constantin Frantz, and perhaps of certain *Grossdeutsch-* and *Trias-politiker* such as Pfordten and Beust,[2] to whom he himself refers. The great publicist Frantz was the most spirited contemporary critic of Bismarck and of the national unification movements of that age; his theory of federalism contained something of a moral-religious self-examination in a century of technical civilization. Yet he erred so often in his political prophecies, mixed so much of the romantically fantastic into his political plans, that one is reluctant to agree with him even in those individual predictions that appear to have been belatedly confirmed, such as in his study of 1859 concerning the European equilibrium. Even there one detects in him the literateur, the pure doctrinaire who stays miles away from any practical responsibility and who, because of his far-reaching perspectives, can no longer recognize the road lying immediately ahead.

It is always futile to dispute over that which did not actually occur in the effort to determine whether it could perhaps have occurred, for there can never be certainty in such a matter. The only concrete attempt at a Central European federation in Bismarck's time such as that put forth by Schnabel was, so far as I can see, Franz Joseph's project at the Congress of Princes in Frankfurt in 1863. Does Schnabel really believe that

[2] As ministers of Bavaria and Saxony, Ludwig von der Pfordten and Friedrich von Beust, advocated a reorganization of the German Confederation on a tripartite (*trias*) basis. Under this plan the lesser states would have had an equal voice with Austria and Prussia in the affairs of the Confederation.—*Ed.*

anything viable and workable could have emerged from this strangely disjointed constitutional plan? To me, the project, with its uncoordinated and inoperable constitutional organs looks like organized impotence—a genuine solution of neither the issue of unity nor that of freedom. Constantin Frantz stressed more strongly than anyone else the belief that a modern parliament was incompatible with the basic principle of a federalized central Europe; such a federation was only conceivable as a union of monarchical governments. It is conceivable, to be sure, that some kind of corporate representative body, more or less on the old Frankish pattern, could have been devised as a substitute for a modern parliament. Perhaps there were other plans for a federation better than that proposed in 1863, plans that never became politically significant. But how can their realization be imagined? A central European federation capable of withstanding the pressure of the eastern and western world powers better than did the Bismarck Reich and its ally Austria-Hungary would have had to possess a superior concentration of strength—a structure, so to speak, of world-power dimensions. Would this not have heightened European tensions very markedly? How carefully Bismarck had to prepare the ground diplomatically for the state he created, deliberately halting in 1866 at the Main River! By contrast, how fantastic seem the plans of a Frantz, who wished his central European federation to include even the smaller border states from Scandinavia through Holland and Belgium to Switzerland, on occasion even Italy—and all of this with the benevolent support of England!

Perhaps Schnabel will reply to this that a central European federation created at the right time would have prevented Germany from ever appearing as a threat to the new world powers. But how is this to be understood? Would Germany's best protection have lain in its weakness? Schnabel could reply that the federation of monarchical-conservative states in central Europe would have resisted national movements of the kind that developed in Italy, Germany, and Western Europe and taken care that such movements did not gain greater strength in the east and southeast; this would have so reduced the dangers for us that we would no longer have had any need for forming a modern national power-state (*Machtstaat*) on German soil. But was there any assurance of this? Had not the decisive impetus for the national movement already been given in 1848, especially in Hungary and Italy? And was it actually sensible to burden the German constitutional problem, which was already hopelessly complicated, with all the unforeseeable needs of the nationalities in the Danube region? Would that not have led to a policy of half solutions, of eternal compromises—to a policy that resisted the whole powerful national current of the century? It seems to me that this strictly monarchical federation of princes would, whether rightly or wrongly, have very quickly been burdened with the same curse of reactionary impotence that hampered the Metternich system before the March revolution of 1848. In spite of all the conjuring up of the old Reich traditions (or perhaps because of it) such a federation would have been regarded as a feudal, artificial makeshift of princely authority. I am not at all satisfied that it would have been better "rooted in the people" than Bismarck's Reich. Above all, I am utterly unable to see how Bismarck could have brought

about this new central European structure through an arch-Prussian particularist like William I, unless it resulted
in some kind of concrete gain in power
for Prussia, instead of mere sacrifices for
the benefit of the medium-sized and
small states.

In my opinion the entire debate is
hopelessly confused by the idea, chiefly
propagated through the works of Srbik,[3]
that the *kleindeutsch* Reich founded in
1866 was chiefly responsible for the internal collapse of the multinational state
on the Danube. Certainly the exclusion
of Austria from the new Reich weakened the position of the Austrian Germans in the Dual Monarchy. However,
it is highly unlikely and impossible to
prove that their hegemony in the army
and bureaucracy could have been maintained indefinitely, or that they would
have been able to solve the nationalities
problem peacefully while maintaining
their old dominance. On the contrary,
the collapse would most certainly have
occurred much earlier if the mighty
power of the Reich that Bismarck created had not buttressed the Vienna monarchy for a long time. Nevertheless, the
end came with the collapse after the unfortunate outcome of World War I. But
the story ended neither in 1914 nor in
1918, and the disintegration of Austria-
Hungary, painful though it was, ought
not to be evaluated entirely as a misfortune, whether seen from either the
European or the German standpoint.
Even Bismarck always treasured the
Dual Monarchy as a dam against Pan-
Slavism, and it would not be easy for
anyone to praise the "Balkanization" of
the Danube region as a masterpiece of

the "peacemakers" of 1919. But did it
not unchain many slumbering forces?
Germany lost at that time not only an
ally but a heavy burden on its foreign
policy as well. The so-called "succession
states" were inimical to Germany in the
beginning, but they were even more
worried about a Russia gone Bolshevik.
A wise, calm, and long-range German
policy offered the best chances, economic and political, for developing a
relationship of mutual trust and fruitful
exchange with these southeastern states,
and for building a peaceful central Europe as Europe's natural barrier against
Bolshevism. This chance was greatly increased after the march into Vienna in
1938 but, almost in the same moment,
it was thrown away.

I think we should look back on the
history of German unification in the
nineteenth century from this point
rather than from 1918. German unification belongs in the great stream of a
European movement which sprang, after
all, not from Germany but from the
French Revolution. The political awak-
ening of peoples was inevitably followed
by the emergence of pressures for national unity, but also for power and
self-realization. Bismarck kept himself
out of this current and even fought
against it in 1848 and afterward with
impassioned zeal, but he finally had to
recognize it as irresistible. If he had attempted to contain it with a romantic-
archaic structure such as Constantin
Frantz designed in his writings—that is,
a central European league of princes
forming a front against both Russia and
France, and with a hand outstretched
toward England—I fear he would be
laughed at today as a strange utopian.
Instead, Bismarck never surrendered to
the national current; actually he toyed
much more seriously and much longer

[3] Heinrich Ritter von Srbik, Austrian historian, whose study of the problem of German
unity is listed in the bibliography of this book.
—*Ed.*

with the idea of a peaceful dualism, of a common Prussian-Austrian domination of Germany (and, indeed, domination in a strict monarchical sense) than was earlier realized. In the end he did not dam the great stream, but utilized it for his own ends. That the national state which he created stopped for the time being at the Main and later at the *kleindeutsch* frontiers can be condemned as a shortcoming from the standpoint of the Austrian Germans or of the south German medium states. Yet it was not an arbitrary act, but one required by the European situation and unavoidable in view of the experiences of 1848–1849.

Schnabel finds it "inconsistent" that Bismarck realized the concept of the national state in Germany while seeking to preserve a dynastic-supranational state structure as long as possible in Austria-Hungary. But his Reich constitution was not at all centralistic along the lines advocated by the unitarian liberals. The virtue of a statesman, moreover, is to be found not in doctrinaire consistency but in the pursuit of practical possibilities. An attempt to solve the domestic problems of the Hapsburg Empire either from Berlin or from Frankfurt or from any other German center would have been presumptuous. It was enough that the Dual Alliance of 1879 gave to the Hapsburg state such a long lease on life, undisturbed by warlike events, that it might well have solved its general internal problems had they been soluble at all. Bismarck was willing to make its existence secure against external dangers but not to support imperialistic plans of conquest in the southeast. That his successors extended the German guarantee unlimitedly, in a truly "*grossdeutsch*" sense, nearly cost Germany its life. Austria-Hungary was responsible for its own ruin. But not even then was "central Europe" lost. Bismarck's idea of creating first a narrow, firm nucleus of power, in which the states of the Danube region could have found firm backing, again had a chance of proving its worth in the twentieth century. In fact, the chance was then for the first time a bright one. But now the German leadership lacked exactly that which was Bismarck's strength: the political acumen, the moral wisdom, the capacity for wise moderation. Hence everything went to pieces in the end, but in spite of Bismarck rather than because of him. A later generation has no right to complain of the "short duration" of his creation, particularly since the period from 1871 to 1914 was after all one of the longest periods of peace in European history.

HERBERT MICHAELIS (1904–   ) was one of the editors of an important collection of German diplomatic documents from the period of Bismarck, *Die auswärtige Politik Preussens 1858–1871* (Berlin, 1932–1939). In 1952 he published a long interpretative essay in a German periodical in which he argues that the Prussian victory over Austria at Königgrätz (also known as Sadowa) in 1866 was the "turning point" in modern German history. This essay, which has attracted little attention, contains some very penetrating observations that bear on the issues debated by Schnabel and Ritter.*

Königgrätz, 1866: Defeat of Liberalism and Universalism

Sadowa meant the victory of the idea of the state in Germany over the concept of federalism, the triumph of undivided power. The ideal of the national state was victorious over the ideal of universal monarchy, the Prussian-German nation over an Austrian-German confederation of "nationalities." There is much justification for saying that it was actually at this point that the old Empire of the Germans came to an end, through the struggle between the federal universalism which was its heritage and the centralistic principle of the modern national state.

The Prussian Junker with his military state had suddenly elevated himself to the status of ruler and representative of Germany. The hopes and expectations, the anxieties and fears aroused by the decision in Bohemia, stemmed from the display of Prussian power rather than from the agitation of German national sentiment. The latter now experienced a powerful upsurge, but at the same time revealed that it was limited to the liberal bourgeois. The question now was not that of 1848, namely into what form the German people would actually translate their demands for national unity and freedom. Rather, it was what Prussia would do with its power and with the national movement, whether it would transform Germany in accordance with the wishes of the nationalists and liberals or whether its only intention

---

* From Herbert Michaelis, "Königgrätz, Eine geschichtliche Wende," *Die Welt als Geschichte*, vol. 12 (1952), pp. 180–192, omitting most of the original footnotes. Translated by Otto Pflanze. By permission of the author.

was selfishly to increase its territory and its domination. The question was soon answered. Prussia did not wish to dissolve into Germany and to sacrifice to Germany its existence as a state. Powerfully fortified by its conquests in the region of northern Germany, it wished to dictate the political structure of non-Austrian Germany, "to dictate to the Germans what their constitution should be" from the standpoint of a conservative-monarchical power whose diminishing vitality had been given new strength through the victory over Austria. In this sense, Königgrätz meant the victory of the state over the nation. The Prussian solution, not the German, dominated the situation. Coming after the rejection of the revolutionary imperial crown in 1849, which destroyed the work of the Paulskirche, Königgrätz meant the renewed victory of the Prussian state over German national liberalism, the reactionary triumph of monarchism over bourgeois democracy, and the disarming of the German revolution.

Along with the fading away of the ancient and genuine concept of empire, the Prussian victory brought to an end the practical projects of reform through which the attempt had been made to master the problem of German political reorganization. All these projects shared the idea of holding on to that region in which the history and fate of the German people had unfolded. In other respects—in aim, motivation, and interest —they diverged radically from one another. In the 1860s, even just a few weeks before the war, the vain attempt had been made to re-establish, on the now questionable basis of German and European conservatism, the harmonious relationship that had existed between Prussia and Austria during the first half of the century. The later so-called Three

Emperor's League, and especially the alliance of 1879, though still animated by a sense of German confederacy, were essentially different in character from the old relationship. . . .

The results of the war brought to the surface once more all the frictions and passions that had aroused the German public when the danger of war first appeared in the spring of 1866.

The defenders of the principle of legitimacy saw that they had erred in expecting that the common threat of the revolutionary *Zeitgeist* would prevent the wielders of power from making warlike decisions. They became witnesses of an unprecedented drama: a highly conservative government made itself the bearer of the dreaded revolution, propagated a general parliament of the people, and unscrupulously brought about the fall of "old and venerated dynasties that stood in the way of its need for power." A king had made revolution. This fact horrified those of legitimist and conservative conviction no less than did the popular forces of democracy.

The old reproach was heard again that Prussia's will to power neglected and destroyed German cultural life. The military spirit and unconditional organization that distinguished the Prussian character aroused fearful respect and antipathy in the rest of Germany. In the intellectual world many looked back with nostalgia on a bygone age in which "nothing had yet been Prussianized"; they praised the former recognition of variety, multiplicity, and the motley in contrast to the current drive for unity and power. Nowadays, observed Jakob Burckhardt, anyone who does not belong to an empire of thirty millions cries, "Lord help us; we are going to ruin."

Since people of this political orientation had no concept of a national renewal of progressive character, the contrast between the old and the new circumstances aroused in them a lively sensitivity for what the war had cost, for the demolition and surrender of a historic region and of the significant power that the vanished German Confederation had possessed despite its organizational and national inadequacies. It had never been attacked by any country. In retrospect, it even appeared as though the German Confederation, by the fact of its existence, had preserved the peace through fifty long years. Now the dream of a German Empire of seventy millions in the heart of Europe had vanished and, with Austria's surrender of Venice, Germany had lost the last element of its position as a world power.

It was generally felt that there never could be a Germany without Austria, that Austria in some form or other must be included in a united Empire if it should ever be formed. This was the only conviction that found an echo also in northern Germany, among the Prussian conservatives. This was so because many contemporaries looked upon the Hapsburg dynasty as the only bond, "that joined the German present with its greater past." But it appeared hopeless to renew the old efforts of the *Grossdeutschen* immediately, and to strive for a German constitution that would provide for union with Austria, or at least its German provinces. One could only hope, as a Bavarian circular dispatch of November 5, 1866, expressed it, that the gap opened by war between Austria and Prussia would gradually be closed, that no ineradicable animosity would replace their earlier comradeship, and that an alliance between the two powers would remain possible. "This wish is all that remains of the previous German union."

The civil war was a shattering experience for Germans. It was no accident that the campaign of 1866 did not give birth to any song. "Silently and sorrowfully German poetry saw its sons destroy one another." The Hapsburg Empire, which lost its position in Italy and Germany, received the blow from which it was ultimately to expire.

There were those who recognized this and expressed it. A few days after the conclusion of the preliminary peace of Nikolsburg, Mayor Giskra of Brünn reacted to the news of Austria's exclusion from Germany by saying to the Prussian Crown Prince, "Austria cannot concede that without signing its own death warrant. Austria exists only through Germany." And Biegeleben, the imperial counsellor who was one of the most determined foes of Prussia in Vienna, broke into tears as he reported on the terms of the Peace of Prague. He was convinced that the treaty which forced the withdrawal of Austria from Germany would be the first Austria would not keep, because it could not do so.

The idea of a centralistic, Germanizing Greater Austria, as conceived by Schwarzenberg and Schmerling, was gone beyond recall. The loss of Austria's position in Germany also weakened the Vienna government internally and made impossible the attempt to establish a unitary, German-dominated general constitution for the monarchy. In place of the external dualism with Prussia appeared the internal dualism between German Austria and Hungary, which destroyed the unitary state. Six months after Königgrätz the Hofburg was compelled to grant the fateful "Settlement." It meant the contraction of German rule to the region of Cisleithania, leaving the region of Transleithania to the Hungarians. . . .

As the German national state, or

"Reich," came into being, the rule of the Germans in the great colonial region of the east dwindled. The old German sense of mission toward southeastern Europe, which was consciously alive and effective until 1866, lapsed into impotence. Thus the defeat at Königgrätz weakened Austria's eastern position, which Bismarck had repeatedly advised it to strengthen as compensation for the renunciation of its position in Germany. For the sake of the principle of nationality, Germany withdrew into its confining inner core. The geographical concept of Germany was narrowed. Slowly the Austrian Germans fell victim to Slavicization and uninhibited Magyarization.

The "Settlement" did not heal and "rejuvenate" the monarchy, as its most determined protagonist, Baron von Beust, expected. Beust's purpose was to bring Austria back into the political game as soon as possible. By utilizing the *grossdeutsch* idea and by allying, if possible, with Napoleon III, he hoped to reverse the result of Königgrätz, hindering the expansion of the North German Confederation under Prussian leadership over the whole of *Kleindeutschland,* and reuniting Austria again with Germany. Because it would solve the most difficult internal problem of the monarchy, the "Settlement" was designed to help him execute this policy.

Contrary to his expectation, however, all kinds of disruptive tendencies became evident within the Hapsburg Empire. The Slavs claimed for themselves the same rights that had been granted the Hungarians. Attendance by Czech nationalists at the Slavic Congress held in Moscow in May 1867 revealed the danger that could emerge from the East. In the Balkan principality of Serbia the movement for liberation of Slavic peoples within the Empire's armed itself for the attack. While the revolution of 1848 had awakened the national consciousness of eastern European peoples, the Prussian victory over Austria now provided them with the opportunity to fight actively for the realization of their national goals. Königgrätz set in motion the whole eastern realm of nationalities, both inside and outside the monarchy, a movement that was never again to cease. Many groups of Germans asked themselves whether the Empire was still necessary for the European balance of power and whether, now that the German national state had been founded, the German provinces of Austria ought to be joined to it. For the first time the possibility arose that the monarchy might one day dissolve and its national elements might "be assimilated by neighboring states to which they were related by nationality and interest." A pamphlet, published by a "German Austrian" in 1867 attempted to prove that the collapse, not the existence of Austria, was a necessity for Europe.

Up to the time of its actual dissolution in 1918 the Danube monarchy was never able to re-establish harmony between its basically German character and the claims of the nationalities. For the time being, to be sure, the *grossdeutsch* hope remained alive. The German Hunters' Festival in Vienna in 1868 was an impressive demonstration for the *grossdeutsch* idea. The assurance that Wilhelm Liebknecht gave at a German workers' convention in Vienna in 1869 that, Königgrätz notwithstanding, "the German workers are one body on both sides of the Austrian frontier and they must be united again in a single Germany" momentarily revived the fading vision. But the reality of political power finally humbled and transformed this attitude. Men reconciled themselves to the *kleindeutsch* unification effected by Prussia. After the defeat of France in 1870–1871 had ruined the last hopes for its destruction and for a "return to Germany," there was a general desire "to proceed together with the new German Reich on the road of the national future," in alliance with it and in recognition of circumstances as they actually were.

The sacrifice required by the decision at Königgrätz was the deepest cleavage within the body of the German people in a thousand years: the Germans of the southeast were henceforth separated from the German motherland. This renunciation of the German position in the southeast was the consequence of ambition for political power. Considered from the historical standpoint, it was a confession of the deterioration of the capacity for empire, of the ability to provide leadership in the region of mixed populations, and a recognition that new forces, new impulses—the national idea and the national state—were on the point of destroying inherited institutions. Through the exclusion of Austria from Germany, the German economy, the German language and culture, were increasingly excluded from their natural sphere of influence in southeastern Europe. With the national concentration of political forces the supranational character of German thought was replaced by a nation-state outlook. Germany lost the will to exert its influence within the wide realm of European culture. Germany itself helped to destroy the spiritual, economic, and political unity of central Europe, which had been essentially German-oriented up to the year of decision, 1866, and through which it had been closely united with Europe as a whole—by political,

and by cultural, Christian bonds. The German course led from the Empire to the State, from the cultural nation to the state-nation and the "monad" of the national state. The Germans of the neighboring states, having lost the last natural connection with the nuclear region, from which, as an "imperial" people, they had originally come, had to rely upon themselves to withstand the growing pressure of alien nationalisms. One can gain an idea of the gigantic historical renunciation and the deterioration of Germany's historical consciousness that was produced by the battle in Bohemia from the fact that, in the midst of World War I, Fredrich Naumann's plan for a united central Europe was received as something completely new. There was no awareness that a half century before Germany had voluntarily surrendered rights in central Europe that were undisputed by the outside world.

Only later was it possible to see clearly that with Prussia's victory (that is, the establishment of a completely self-centered autonomy for the organism of the national state) the German state and people were divested of their historical mediating function. The bond which had joined Germany to Europe was severed and its frontier sharply defined *vis-à-vis* other countries. The goal of Prussian policy was increase in Prussian power and elevation of the Germans to the status of a nation, not service to Europe. With Königgrätz began a transformation of the German moral and political physiognomy and of German political thought which was of the greatest consequence. The transformation of the latter completed beyond recall the exhaustion of the traditional concept of empire, although the attempt was made to revive it in the unhistorical form of the Reich of the national state. It brought about a devaluation of both the universal culture that had borne the old imperial idea and the spiritual heritage of Western liberalism. The continental community of peoples lost a great constituent element of its previous history. With one stroke a completely new, previously unknown Germany was launched. . . .

The forces that fought each other in the Prussian constitutional conflict—authoritarian monarchy and parliamentary liberalism—espoused basically the same goals: to unite Germany into a single state and to make it a powerful force in the political world. The latter was to be achieved through a union between the consciousness of the Prussian-German tradition and the expansionistic tendencies and developmental drive of the bourgeois economy. While the liberals wished to attain unity through freedom and in this desire even saw Prussia as their leader, the interests of Prussian power required that it separate nationalism from liberalism. By fulfilling the desires for national unity, the feudal-conservative, Prussian state that wished to rule Germany could hold the cry for freedom within the limits prescribed by its *raison d'état*. With the help of nationalism, liberalism could be weakened and the traditional social structure maintained, even in a world that had changed and was being changed in so many ways.

The popular struggle of the revolution of 1848 had sought to achieve both unity and freedom. Bismarck's achievement was to separate them, to transform the German problems [of unity and freedom] from parallel into successive problems, and to split the progressive movement. On the day of Königgrätz he achieved this goal. Before the war he remarked to the French ambassador Benedetti,

"However he may think about the issues of freedom, there is a bit of Frederick the Great in every Prussian." And he calculated correctly. As we have seen, however, it was not the glory of military victory alone that brought him this success over the domestic opposition, the kind of glory, he once remarked, permitting one to "achieve everything one wants." It must not be overlooked that a bifurcation had already occurred in the struggle for freedom and unity during the political persecutions of the 1830s. Since that time two groups, which previously had been closely allied, had been fighting one another: one for whom there was "no fatherland without freedom," another for whom there was "no freedom without a fatherland." Their conflict made Bismarck's game easier. He also profited from the awakened national self-confidence, from political and economic expectations, and, as we still have to show, from the friction with foreign countries—all of which permitted the phenomenon of nationalism to triumph over the demands of liberalism. As in England, furthermore, the economic prosperity since about 1850 not only took the wind out of the sails of the radicals but strengthened the opinion that the radicalism of 1830–1848 had been an error altogether. "The economic advantages of unification became more evident at the very moment when the benefits of prosperity made radical reform less urgent."[1]

The favorable economic situation made it easier for Bismarck to separate nationalism from liberalism. It also helped him achieve another epochal separation: conservatism from the principle of legitimism. This double deed meant farewell to the spirits of both

[1] G. Barraclough, *Factors in German History* (Oxford, England, 1946), p. 119.

the eighteenth century and the first half of the nineteenth century. It made possible an alliance between liberal nationalism and conservative nationalism and the development of a specifically German brand of nationalism no longer comparable to that of other countries. German nationalism lost its inner connection with the Enlightenment and the romanticism from which it had sprung; it no longer recognized any supranational bonds. To put it another way, German patriotism became conservative, "with the result that many men who had been liberal because they were patriots became conservative for the same reason." Through the conservative fulfillment of its goals by Bismarck, German liberalism suffered its decisive defeat. An Englishman came to the heart of the matter when he declared that between 1862 and 1871 Bismarck converted a liberal into a conservative nationalism, a humanitarian into a military nationalism, and a democratic into a monarchical nationalism. . . .[2]

Twice, at the two decisive points in Germany's history in the nineteenth century, the people voluntarily and expressly surrendered the affairs of the people to the state. The twin brother of the liberal idea, nationalism, which had been consciously strengthened by Bismarck as a counterweight to liberal and radical demands in the interest of the Prussian state and society, turned against its own liberal past and became an end in itself. This change was made possible and was furthered by the tendency, generally evident since the French Revolution, increasingly to divest the national idea of its cosmopolitan and humanitarian characteristics. It was remolded

instead into a national realism typical of the second half of the nineteenth century, not merely in Germany. This consequence of 1866 was a most decisive phenomenon of modern German history. In it lay a principal root of all future internal German tensions and struggles. It prevented the union of liberal forces with the national idea, just as it permitted the latter, wherever irresponsible men became its leaders, to degenerate into unbridled nationalistic superiority and the criminal denial of freedom and the worth of man. From that time, it was possible in Germany for the noblest idealism and human depravity to appeal equally to the national idea. On the other hand, any genuine striving for freedom that went beyond the limits permitted by the state was regarded as hostile to the state.

To summarize, within Germany Königgrätz meant the victory of reaction over freedom for two more generations. Bourgeois democracy, which had been victorious over feudalism in France and England, was conquered in Germany for the second time by Prussian feudalism, by the counterrevolution. The outcome ensured the continued existence of the authoritarian Hohenzollern monarchy, which in the course of the constitutional conflict had been driven to the verge of surrender. It secured and renewed the social power of the feudal and conservative classes. These classes dominated Prussia politically through their control over the Prussian Landtag with its reactionary three-class electoral system and by their supremacy in the army and bureaucracy. They dominated economically through their agrarian possessions and later through their alliance with the new liberal, bourgeois entrepreneurial class. With the extension of Prussian power in 1866 over northern Germany and in

[2] Bertrand Russell, *Freedom versus Organization, 1814–1914* (New York, 1934), p. 362, 368–382.

1870 over the entire *kleindeutsch* world of states and peoples, these classes became the decisive factors in German life. The bourgeois, satisfied by the winning of unity and by the swelling economic prosperity, experienced a process of depoliticization or, along with other segments from all social classes in Germany, the cultivation of political power as an end in itself. As one German historian, who was too much under the influence of his impressions of 1945, has expressed it, they "took an almost heathen delight in Machiavellian modes of thought," in what the national liberals, using Bismarck's vocabulary, call *"Realpolitik."* On this foundation, Bismarck transformed the German Confederation constitutionally into a federal state and created the North German constitution with the intent of making secure the hegemony of the Junkers and of the upper bourgeois in Prussia, as well as Prussia's position in the Reich.

His deed was to rescue Prussian monarchical absolutism, whose time in history had expired, to preserve it in a greatly altered world, and to expand its spirit throughout the *kleindeutsch* region. In outward form Bismarck's constitution stressed federalism, but in practice it could not in any way influence or jeopardize the hegemony of Prussia. Particularism was "abolished," to be sure, but its end did not mean the transfer of political power from the princes to the German people. Yet the people sanctioned the result. They cheered the Prussian state from which in 1848 they had attempted to coerce unity and freedom and to which they now willingly and helpfully surrendered the task of national unification, renouncing freedom for the second time. The Reichstag was a concession to liberalism, but it was granted much more for tactical reasons than for reasons of principle. "Should the parliament we are summoning have a revolutionary majority," Bismarck remarked in April 1866 to Benedetti, who was concerned over this development, "we will abolish it and destroy the German Confederation; then nothing will prevent Prussia from executing its plan for a North German Confederation." The spirit in which Prussia entered upon its domination of Germany (we may not casually identify it in this form, to be sure, with the spirit of Bismarck) is expressed in the sentences that General von Schleinitz, who rode with the Prussian king through the Bistriz valley on the evening of the battle of Königgrätz, wrote on that very evening: ". . . this was a truly German imperial procession (*Kaiserritt*), . . . which expunges from us the shame of that other one of March 1848 when Frederick William IV went through the farce of appearing with the black-red-gold banner of revolution . . . I said to myself that we have not only conquered the Austrians; we have also solved the German question and thereby disarmed the German revolution. I felt as though a heavy weight had been removed from my breast and I could now breathe freely, confident in the thought that the victorious king would no longer need the support of democratic elements . . ., but could now rule conservatively and respectably."

HELMUT BÖHME (1936–   ) studied at the
University of Hamburg under Fritz Fischer, whose
Griff Nach der Weltmacht, concerning German war
aims in 1914–1918, has become one of the most
controversial books in German historial literature.
In his first book, Böhme takes an equally
unorthodox and controversial position with regard
to German unification. He sees German history
primarily in terms of the ebb and flow of economic life
and of the pressures it creates on politics. Hence
the dates 1866 and 1871 seem to him less important
than those of 1865 and 1873–1879.*

Free Trade, 1865: Prussia's Success Due to Economic Strength

The new political order negotiated for
Europe by the Congress of Vienna
brought no change in the German question. The dualism of the two German
great powers, which had arisen in the
eighteenth century, was not ended. Actually the traditional Prussian policy of
arrondissement[1] was given an additional
dimension, since Prussia entered the new
political order with its "center of gravity
shifted to the west." Its emerging industrial region in the west [the Ruhr]
was separated from the administrative
heart of the state [Berlin]. The first wave

[1] The quest for contiguous territorial possessions and rounded frontiers in order to attain
a more compact state.—*Ed.*

of industrialization and the fact that its
territories were divided produced in
Prussia a strong impulse toward the
formation of a unified territorial state.
This could be achieved either through
direct annexation or through indirect
domination by means of an economic
union between Prussia, Electoral Hesse,
Hanover, and Brunswick. Since Austria
regarded its primacy in Germany as the
basis of its power position in Europe,
Austrian and Prussian policy clashed
with increasing sharpness. And yet open
conflicts were avoided before 1848.

In view of the danger of democratic
and national revolution, Austria and
Prussia agreed in the first half of the

* From Helmut Böhme, *Deutschlands Weg zur Grossmacht, Studien zum Verhältnis von Wirtschaft und Staat während der Reichsgründungszeit, 1848–1881* (Cologne: Verlag Kiepenheur &
Witsch, 1966), pp. 13–17, 211–212, omitting the original footnotes. Translated by Otto Pflanze. By
permission of the author and Verlag Kiepenheuer & Witsch.

nineteenth century, to check the further development of revolutionary ideas and to curb all liberal and national movements in the central European area. Both states renounced any activity with regard to the German question and satisfied themselves with a confederate policy in which each carefully considered the interests of the other. Prussia accepted its seeming position of equality with Austria in the German Confederation and was satisfied with strengthening its economic position. And Austria did not stress its primacy in the German Confederation but concentrated on strengthening its influence on the medium-sized and small states and on blocking the national and liberal movement. Nevertheless, the political order of the Restoration and the tactic of "prior understanding" between the dual powers in the affairs of the Confederation came to an end in 1848. The liberal-national and social movements appeared to be stronger than all the efforts of conservative statesmen to preserve the system of Vienna. The Austrian chancellor Prince Metternich, who was the leader and symbol of the Restoration era, fell with the first assault. The dissolution of the Hapsburg Empire into its national components and the creation of a German Reich, based on a democratic-parliamentary order and including the German-speaking region of the [Hapsburg Empire], appeared to be only a question of time.

Yet force of arms decided otherwise. By the end of 1848 it had become clear that the hopes of the Frankfurt parliament for a *grossdeutsch* Reich had been crushed. In Prussia and in Austria the old order, supported by the army and the bureaucracy, again resumed leadership of the state. In Austria the summoning of Prince Felix Schwarzenberg as minister-president meant above all a firm decision to re-establish the monarchy as a centralized state. At the same time it marked the beginning of an active greater Austrian policy, which rejected all proposals for a constitutional federation and challenged all plans of the Frankfurt assembly for a *grossdeutsch* Reich. The goal of Schwarzenberg was the creation of a greater Austria (*Grossösterreich*), not a greater Germany (*Grossdeutschland*). This greater Austria was to be the "leading power of a central Europe controlled by Austrian Germans." Through such a development he expected to be able to overcome the national movements [which had emerged during the revolution].

The German problem immediately became the focal point of Schwarzenberg's policy. He believed that the consolidation of the internal structure of the Hapsburg monarchy under the leadership of its German provinces required the reduction of Prussian power in Germany.[2] To that end he immediately challenged Prussia's right to "parity" with Austria in the Frankfurt Diet, a right which, although largely fictional, Metternich had always carefully respected. In particular, however, Schwarzenberg challenged Prussia's primacy in

[2] Schwarzenberg's reasoning was as follows: the re-establishment of monarchical authority within the Empire could only be achieved through a governmental centralization which would keep liberal and national movements in check. The policy of centralization had to be based on the German population of the Empire, which staffed the civil service. But the Germans were a minority in the Empire and their rule, to be successful, depended upon the support of the millions of Germans outside the Austrian frontier. To gain that support, Austria had to dominate the German Confederation and Zollverein. Domestic and foreign policy, political and economic affairs were woven together in one grand design, whose fulfillment would have meant Austrian hegemony in central Europe.—*Ed.*

the Zollverein and asserted Austria's claim to leadership in Germany.

Schwarzenberg's Germany policy was novel in that it concentrated more on economic than on political and military affairs. He advanced vigorously the plan for a customs union (Zollunion) between Austria and the Zollverein. This union was to be the nucleus of a central European economic block under Austrian leadership. He stressed to the youthful Kaiser Franz Joseph that this plan was the most important "instrument" for establishing a lasting position of leadership for Austria not only in Germany but throughout the continent. Through this union he hoped to be able to bind together the disparate parts of the monarchy under German-Austrian leadership and to re-establish the parity of the Empire with the other European great powers, all of which had set out to win for themselves world-wide spheres of influence.

Schwarzenberg found strong support for his plans in the minister of commerce, Baron von Bruck. While for Schwarzenberg the immediate power-political aspect of the customs union was decisive, Bruck stressed the economic-political goals of such a union. To be sure, he also saw the political advantages of a powerful commercial alliance in central Europe, but he stressed particularly that Austria's union with the prospering Zollverein would give to the development of its economy a new stimulation that could then be exploited in the power-political sphere. He had Prussia's example in mind when he strove in 1848–1849 to force a way into the Zollverein, which Vienna up to this point had more or less ignored. Nevertheless, in complete contrast to the dominant tendency in the Zollverein the Austrians intended, once they had joined it, to

close off the enlarged Zollverein by erecting protective tariffs against other countries and in this way to adapt it completely to Austrian requirements. The realization of Austrian plans for a customs union would have hampered the growth of the expanding economy of Prussia-Germany, for the Austrian economy was weaker in capital and less favored in natural resources than that of Prussia-Germany. Furthermore, Prussian agriculture, which was interested in export, would have come into immediate competition with Hungarian agriculture, and the latter was favored by lower costs. Politically, the success of the Austrian plans would have robbed Prussia of its power position in Germany and reduced it to the status of the German medium-sized states.

The struggle over the customs union came to be of central importance for the further development of the German problem, and it can be asserted that the *kleindeutsch* national state arose chiefly from the Prussian defense against Austrian plans for a great economic order in central Europe. For, in defending itself against the Schwarzenberg-Bruck conception, Prussia laid the foundation for its own later hegemony.

Prussia's most important weapon in this struggle was its insistence on low tariffs, for Austria could not join a Zollverein based on the principle of free trade. For that reason the preservation of free trade and the continued exclusion of Austria from the Zollverein became in increasing degree the political axiom of Prussian policy in the struggle for supremacy in central Europe.

The only question was whether Prussia could follow a policy of free trade and whether it could win the agreement of the members of the Zollverein to such a policy. Being still an overwhelmingly agrarian country with good transportation to the industrial countries of western Europe, Prussia, in contrast to Austria, was interested in exports. Likewise its manufacturers and its big merchants sought an exchange of goods unrestricted by high internal and external tariffs. Hence a free-trade policy corresponded with their interests. Bruck knew this. But he counted on support from the newly emerging heavy industry in Prussia which, in view of English competition, demanded protective tariffs that corresponded with Austria's plans for central Europe. In the southern and medium-sized states Bruck hoped above all for the support of the textile industrialists.

Yet his calculation proved to be unrealistic. The medium-sized states could not ignore Prussia's economic potency. Furthermore, Prussia dominated the waterways. Despite the pro-Austrian outlook of the governments of the medium-sized states, Prussian commercial policy found increasing support from economic interests throughout Germany. During the course of the struggle between Austria and Prussia, in fact, the liberal and pro-Austrian medium-sized states were drawn increasingly into the orbit of the conservative, pseudo-liberal great power of the north. The economic interests looked to Prussia and not to Austria as the leading power in Germany. This limited the freedom of political action of the medium-sized states very considerably. All plans for a third force were condemned to failure from the outset. During the struggle over the plan designed by Austria to fortify its power position in Germany and Europe, therefore, the Danube monarchy became evermore isolated within Germany.

In Prussia the leaders of heavy industry were sympathetic to the plans of Bruck, but their political influence was not yet effective, in contrast to the Prussian and German pressure groups of manufacturers and traders, and especially those east Elbian agrarians who were interested in the export of grain and liquors made from sugar beets. The option of the Rhenish liberal upper-middle class for the "state of Frederick William IV" and for the religious, patriarchal, and conservative order of Prussia (which came about as a reaction to the economic crisis of the year 1848 and the June uprising of the workers in Paris) had created a new alignment in Prussia which was of great importance for the political development of Germany in the nineteenth century. Out of the common economic interests shared by traders, bankers, and industrialists, on the one hand, and the conservative, agrarian-feudal leading class of Prussia, on the other, there arose a new political coalition based on the liberal principle of free trade and maintenance of the status quo. Those Rhenish and Silesian entrepreneurs who were building up an industrial-capitalistic economic system also needed "peace and order." For this reason they allied themselves with the east Elbians and minimized their economic and commercial demands. This combination of interests wrecked not only the liberal-democratic onset of the "revolution" of 1848, but also the plans of the Austrians.

The conflict between the two German great powers had yet another consequence in Prussia. During this conflict the Prussian upper-middle class largely lost its political weight. The result was that the liberal-conservative bureaucracy was bound ever more closely to the traditional leading class of the Prussian state. It was a peculiarity of Prussian development that the aristocracy remained so strong and unbroken that it could divert the pressures and dynamism of the entrepreneurial middle class into the channel of its own political interests and that it was capable of making the transition to a capitalistic, large-scale agriculture. Thus the coalition between the agrarians and the property-owning middle class (especially the big merchants) was characterized after 1849 by a "division of labor": the leading businessmen recognized the ‧ traditional political leaders and the latter left the economic leadership largely to the middle class. Through this symbiosis with the bourgeoisie the nobility was able to hold on to its threatened position. The nobility even succeeded in taming the industrial entrepreneurs politically—in view of the rising menace of social revolution.

Seen from the standpoint of the quarrel over the economic-political domination of central Europe and over its economic order, the summoning of Bismarck to the minister-presidency of Prussia and the period of parliamentary conflict in 1862–1863 represents only an accentuation of the political struggle. It was, however, no hiatus in Prussia's progress toward hegemonial power in Germany. Before the war with Austria began in 1866 the commercial-political struggle for Germany had already been decided. In accordance with the economic basis of political development, the most important result of the treaties of Nikolsburg and Prague was, next to the annexations north of the Main, Prussia's attainment of freedom of decision in matters of trade policy. This was accomplished through nonrenewal of the central European treaty of 1853[3] and

through formation of a closed national economic region by means of the reconstruction of the Zollverein.

Industrial expansion and economic reconstruction left their imprint on the political development of Germany in the nineteenth century. The trend they produced toward the formation of larger trading areas, the financial necessities of the German states, and especially the superiority of Prussian diplomacy forced the small and medium-sized states of north and south Germany into economic and, ultimately, political cooperation with Prussia. All plans for a federal union of medium-sized states remained utopian. Economic development oriented the medium-sized states toward Prussia. For that reason Delbrück, Philipsborn, Manteuffel, Schweinitz, Schleinitz, Bernstorff, and particularly Bismarck very consciously made Prussia's tariff system a lever of Prussian foreign policy. Prussian foreign policy and Prussian commercial policy were inextricably interwoven in the struggle for supremacy in Germany and in central Europe. Hence the achievement of the free trade system in the Zollverein meant the establishment of Prussia's supremacy in Germany and of Prussia as a great power. While sparing Austria, Bismarck attained in the Peace of Prague the "war aims" within Germany that buttressed and fortified this development. These were the constitution of the North German Confederation, the offensive and defensive alliances with the south German states, and the geopolitical *arrondissement* of Prussia through the annexation of Hanover, Electoral Hesse, Frankfurt, and Nassau. With the liquidation of the "gulden center" (Frankfurt), the taler conquered the gulden. At the same time Austria was reoriented toward the

---

[3] The treaty of February 19, 1853 between Austria and the Zollverein permitted Austria to reopen after 1860 the issue of establishing a tariff union with the Zollverein.—*Ed.*

Balkans and the latent tension between the two eastern empires (Austria and Russia) was utilized to establish for Prussia an independent, mediating role.

The success of the conservative statesman Bismarck made possible a final settlement with the liberal leaders. The Prussian-Germany economy flourished; the adherents of a German unitary state believed Bismarck to be "their man." This was the reason for the carefully considered conciliatory attitude of Prussian leadership toward wishes of the liberals. Without actually giving the liberals real political power, Bismarck understood how to admit them to influential consultation, and how to dull their personal political ambitions while fulfilling their economic-political demands. Simultaneously the change in the relationship between state and individual, which Stein and Hardenberg had initiated, was brought to an end. This change was characterized by the dissolution of the "principle of direction." It began with the abolition of hereditary servitude (1807) and reached its completion with the grant of freedom of domicile and freedom of occupation (1868). With these statutes the "authoritarian state" relinquished its final power of intervention in the ever more complicated relationships of production. The state now limited itself to regulating the conditions under which business enterprises existed and competed with one another.

The victory of Prussian arms, and the political changes and economic-political results that stemmed from it, were the starting point for a period of brilliant prosperity. In 1870–1871 this upsurge in economic activity was stimulated anew by the victory over France and by France's payment of a war indemnity of billions. Yet the founding of the German Reich produced no interruption in the development of the economy or of commercial policy. From the economic standpoint the years 1866–1876 can be considered as a single unit; as a period characterized by the dominance of commercial and agrarian interests in the legislation of Prussia and of the German states. During this decade, however, the first signs of a change appeared. The rise in prosperity brought heavy industry steadily into the foreground of Prussian-German economic life. The influence of the hitherto dominant interests (the feudal aristocracy and middle-class traders) was constantly restricted. Hence the economic crisis of 1873 became a crisis of power relationships in Prussia and Germany. During this crisis the liberals and their "leaders"—Delbrück, Camphausen, and Bennigsen—were ruined by the new solidarity between industry, agriculture, and the conservative system that resulted from the crisis.

The creation of the Imperial Bank, the emergence of the interest groups, the resignation of Delbrück, and Bismarck's complete reversion to the forces of conservatism brought to an end the period in which a conservative Prussia established its ascendancy over Austria and Germany by means of the liberal principles and interests of autonomous free trade. Already Europe felt the superior weight of a united mid-continental state. The traditional pentarchy of European politics threatened to collapse.

Suggestions for Additional Reading

The literature on Bismarck and German unification is one of the most voluminous on any subject in the history of modern Europe. Among German writers this period has aroused as keen an interest as American historians have shown in the Civil War, a contemporaneous event. Unfortunately most of the works have never been translated into English, which will handicap many students who wish to pursue further some of the issues raised in this book. The literature in English, however, is considerable, as many English and American historians, too, have been interested in the period because of its importance for modern history.

The most authoritative survey of German history since the Reformation is Hajo Holborn, *A History of Modern Germany* (3 vols.; 1959–1967); the last volume covers the period since 1840. For a brief account, see Walter Simon, *Germany: A Brief History* (New York, 1966), which contains an annotated bibliography of the literature in English. The best general history by German authors is Otto Brandt, Arnold O. Meyer, and Leo Just, eds., *Handbuch der deutschen Geschichte*; vol. 3, no. 3, *Das Zeitalter Bismarcks* (Constance, 1955), is by Walter Bussmann. A standard work on the nineteenth and twentieth centuries is Koppel S. Pinson, *Modern Germany, Its History and Civilization* (New York, 1954), the second edition of which (1966) contains chapters by Klaus Epstein and an extensive bibliography of books in English.

The period of unification is treated in detail in many volumes. An "official" history,

written while Bismarck was still in office, is Heinrich von Sybel, *Founding of the German Empire by William I* (7 vols.; New York, 1890–1898). Other works written from the Prussian standpoint are Erich Brandenburg, *Die Reichsgründung* (2 vols.; Leipzig, 1922), Erich Marcks, *Der Aufstieg des Reiches* (2 vols.; Stuttgart, 1936), and Otto Becker, *Bismarcks Ringen um Deutschlands Gestaltung* (Heidelberg, 1958). The Austrian point of view is presented by Heinrich Friedjung, *The Struggle for Supremacy in Germany, 1859–1866* (New York, 1935) and by Heinrich Ritter von Srbik, *Deutsche Einheit* (4 vols.; Munich, 1935–1942). A critical interpretation by a liberal historian is Johannes Ziekursch, *Politische Geschichte des neuen Deutschen Kaiserreiches* (3 vols.; Frankfurt, 1925–1930); vol. 1 deals with the unification period. An important study concentrating primarily on the years 1850–1863 is Egmont Zechlin, *Die Grundlegung der deutschen Grossmacht* (Stuttgart, 1930). Recently Helmut Böhme has added a new dimension to the problem in his *Deutschlands Weg zur Grossmacht, Studien zum Verhältnis von Wirtschaft und Staat während der Reichsgründungszeit, 1848–1881* (Cologne, 1966), which studies the period from the standpoint of economic and social history and its relationship to state policy. Still useful, though somewhat dated, is Adolphus W. Ward and Spenser Wilkinson, *Germany, 1815–1890* (3 vols.; Cambridge, Eng., 1916–1918).

The various interpretations of the German revolution in 1848 are discussed fruitfully in an article by Theodore S. Hamerow, "History and the German Revolution of 1848," *American Historical Review* LX (1954), 27–44. The most detailed, indeed exhaustive, history of the revolution is that of Veit Valentin, *Geschichte der deutschen Revolution von 1848–1849* (2 vols.; Berlin, 1930–1931). The one-volume English abridgment of this work, *1848: Chapters in German History* (London, 1940), reflects some of the defects of the original, namely its encyclopedic character and lack of clear organization. By contrast, Rudolf Stadelmann succeeds much better in presenting the same liberal viewpoint in his *Soziale und politische Geschichte der Revolution von 1848* (Munich, 1948). Still significant is the older study by Erich Brandenburg, *Die deutsche Revolution* (Leipzig, 1912), which shows an awareness of economic and social aspects of the revolution that is lacking in many later German works. These aspects are dealt with almost exclusively in Theodore S. Hamerow's *Restoration, Revolution, Reaction: Economics and Politics in Germany, 1815–1871* (Princeton, N.J., 1958). Despite its broad title, the short work of Sir Lewis Namier, *1848: The Revolution of the Intellectuals* (London, 1945) concentrates almost entirely on the subject of nationalism, in particular on the nationalistic attitudes displayed in the Frankfurt parliament. Of the many works inspired by the centenary of the revolution, the best is probably that of Stadelmann, but see also Wilhelm Mommsen, *Grösse und Versagen des deutschen Bürgertums, Ein Beitrag zur Geschichte der Jahre 1848–1849* (Stuttgart, 1949); Theodor Heuss, *1848, Werk und Erbe* (Stuttgart, 1948); and Friedrich Meinecke, *1848—Eine Säkularbetrachtung* (Berlin, 1949). Documentary materials that help to bring the age alive are contained in Karl Obermann, *Einheit und Freiheit, Die deutsche Geschichte von 1814–1849 in zeitgenössischen Dokumenten* (Berlin, 1950).

Some idea of the amount of literature on Bismarck can be gained from Karl E. Born, ed., *Bismarck-Bibliographie, Quellen und Literatur zur Geschichte Bismarcks und seiner Zeit* (Cologne, 1966), which contains 6138 entries, yet has been criticized as incomplete. Useful as bibliographical guides are the articles by Lawrence Steefel, "Bismarck," in *Journal of Modern History*, II (1930), 74–95; Andreas Dorpalen, "The German Historians and Bismarck," *Review of Politics*, XV (1953), 53–67; and G. P. Gooch, "The Study of Bismarck," in *Studies in German History* (London, 1948), pp. 301–341. Biographies began to appear even before the chancellor's career had ended and lately the rate has been about one each year. Yet only one author has achieved what can be described as a full-scale biography: Erich Eyck, *Bismarck, Leben und Werk* (3 vols.; Zurich, 1941–1944), of which a one-volume English abridgment has appeared, *Bismarck and the German Empire* (London, 1950). Eyck's viewpoint is critical, but this cannot be said of the biography by Arnold O. Meyer, *Bismarck, Der Mensch und der Staatsmann* (Stuttgart, 1949), which was written during the same years and published only after the author's death. For other eulogistic biographies, see Ludwig Reiners, *Bismarck* (2 vols.; Munich, 1956–1957) and Wilhelm Mommsen, *Bismarck, Ein politisches Lebensbild* (Munich, 1959). English and American studies of Bismarck have tended to be more critical than German ones. Otto Pflanze, *Bismarck and the Development of Germany: The Period of Unification, 1815–1871* (Princeton, 1963) is the first of a projected two-volume analysis of Bismarck's impact upon the course of German political life. An acceptable brief biography is W. N. Medlicott, *Bismarck and Modern Germany* (Mystic, Conn., 1965). Less reliable in interpretation and detail are A. J. P. Taylor, *Bismarck: the Man and the Statesman* (London, 1955) and Werner Richter, *Bismarck* (New York, 1965), the latter being a somewhat abridged translation of a German work published in 1962. Other English works are F. Darmstaedter, *Bismarck and the Creation of the Second Reich* (London, 1948) and Charles G. Robertson, *Bismarck* (London, 1918). The best study of Bismarck's early years and development is Erich Marcks, *Bismarcks Ju-*

gend, 1815–1848 (Stuttgart, 1909), which was to have been the first in a multivolume biography that was never completed. Finally, the student can gain a vivid, although not always accurate, picture of Bismarck from his memoirs, translated as *Bismarck: The Man and the Statesman* (2 vols.; New York, 1899). The definitive edition of this work, dictated by Bismarck after his retirement, is edited by Gerhard Ritter as Volume 15 of *Bismarck Die Gesammelten Werke,* 15 vols.; (Berlin, 1924–1935).

The monographic and periodical literature on Bismarck and the period of unification is rich in content and controversy. The views of Hans Rothfels are best portrayed in *Bismarck, Der Osten und das Reich* (Stuttgart, 1960), *Bismarck und der Staat* (Stuttgart, 1954), "Problems of a Bismarck Biography," *Review of Politics,* IX (1947), 362–380, "Bismarck und das neunzehnte Jahrhundert," in Walther Hubatsch, ed., *Schicksalswege deutscher Vergangenheit* (Düsseldorf, 1950), pp. 233–248, "1848—One Hundred Years After," *Journal of Modern History,* XX (1948), 291–319, and "On Occasion of the 150th Anniversary of the Birthday of Bismarck," *Universitas,* vol. 8 (1965), pp. 9–22. For the general interpretation of Gerhard Ritter see *Europa und die deutsche Frage* (Munich, 1948) and *Staatskunst und Kriegshandwerk, Das Problem des "Militarismus" in Deutschland,* vol. 1 (Munich, 1954). The problem of Bismarck's moral and religious convictions has received considerable attention, and there is an extensive literature on this subject alone. Typical of the contrasting views are the fairly critical article by Hajo Holborn on "Bismarck's Realpolitik" reprinted in this volume and the eulogistic monograph of Leonhard von Muralt, *Bismarcks Verantwortlichkeit* (Göttingen, 1955).

The controversy that Franz Schnabel aroused when he published the views presented in this volume can be found in the following articles: Franz Schnabel, "Bismarck und die Nationen," *La Nouvelle Clio,*

I-II (1949–1950), 87–102, also printed in *Europa und der Nationalismus* (Baden-Baden, 1950), pp. 91–108, "Bismarck und die klassische Diplomatie," *Aussenpolitik,* III (1952), 635–642, and "Das Problem Bismarck," *Hochland,* XLII (1949), translated as "The Bismarck Problem" in Hans Kohn ed., *German History: Some New German Views* (London, 1954), pp. 65–93; Gerhard Ritter, "Grossdeutsch und Kleindeutsch im 19. Jahrhundert," in W. Hubatsch, ed., *Schicksalswege deutscher Vergangenheit* (Düsseldorf, 1950) pp. 177–201 and "Das Bismarckproblem," *Merkur,* IV, no. 1, (1950), 657–676; Wilhelm Schüssler, "Noch einmal: Bismarck und die Nationen," *La Nouvelle Clio,* I-II (1949–1950), 432–455, and *Um das Geschichtsbild* (Gladbeck, 1953), pp. 102–122; Heinrich Ritter von Srbik, "Die Bismarck-Kontroverse," *Wort und Wahrheit,* no. 2, (1950), 918–931; and Otto Pflanze, "Bismarck and German Nationalism," *American Historical Review,* LX (1955), 548–566.

The war of 1870–1871 has produced a monographic literature of its own. In addition to the works by Oncken, Dittrich, and Eyck represented by selections in this book, the student can consult with profit the text and documents published by Robert H. Lord, *The Origins of the War of 1870* (Cambridge, Mass., 1924). After World War II a number of new documents became available and were published by Georges Bonnin, ed., *Bismarck and the Hohenzollern Candidature for the Spanish Throne, The Documents in the German Diplomatic Archives* (London, 1957) and Ernest Walder, ed., *Die Emser Depesche* (Bern, 1959). A judicious study of the problem on the basis of all these materials is Lawrence D. Steefel, *Bismarck, The Hohenzollern Candidacy, and the Origins of the Franco-German War of 1870* (Cambridge, 1962). Earlier, Steefel published a classic study of the war of 1864, *The Schleswig-Holstein Question* (Cambridge, Mass., 1932). *DIPLOMACY IN IRON: The Life of Herbert von Bismarck,* by Louis L. Snyder (Krieger Publishing, Malabar, Florida, 1985).